FIVE MINUTES LOVE

FIVE MINUTES LOVE

CAROL HATHORNE

ISIS
LARGE PRINT
Oxford

Copyright © Carol Hathorne, 2006

First published in Great Britain 2006
by
The Kates Hill Press

Published in Large Print 2008 by ISIS Publishing Ltd.,
7 Centremead, Osney Mead, Oxford OX2 0ES
by arrangement with
the Author

British Library Cataloguing in Publication Data
Hathorne, Carol
    Five minutes love. – Large print ed.
    (Isis reminiscence series)
    1. Hathorne, Carol
    2. Large print books
    3. Tipton (England) – Social life and customs
    – 20th century
    4. Tipton (England) – Biography
    I. Title
    942.4'94085'092

ISBN 978–0–7531–9474–4 (hb)
ISBN 978–0–7531–9475–1 (pb)

Printed and bound in Great Britain by
T. J. International Ltd., Padstow, Cornwall

Carol Hathorne is the author of 18 published books. She was born in Tipton in 1944 and has lived in the Black Country all her life. Her early novels appeared under the name Carol Marsh.

FOR

My brother, Dave.

Acknowledgements

I should like to thank my husband Mark for his love and encouragement.
Special thanks also to Greg Stokes and the Kates Hill Press for showing such interest in my work.

CONTENTS

SLURRY AND STRAWBERRIES

CHAPTER
ONE

Big Aunt Ginny pulled your teeth out. I tried not to remember how she'd done it to me, as I watched her, vigorously scrubbing my little brother's hot and dirty face with a soap dampened corner of her apron.

"Keep still, yer little bugger!" The "clank-clank" of her wedding ring against his open mouth was drowned as he gasped and squirmed and finally began to bellow his protests.

"Aaargh! That hurts! I'll tell me Mom!"

Big Aunt Ginny's long, gaunt face scowled. She didn't answer, but her grip tightened on Dave's flailing arms, effectively pinning him down onto the scrubbed top table as she grimly applied the green "Sunlight" and cold water.

Standing forgotten by the back door, I trembled in the atmosphere of tension and danger that always came descending, when our mother went away.

Big Aunt Ginny didn't like us. I knew it with a deep, eight year olds' instinctive certainty. It was because she didn't like us that she used her wedding ring as a face scraper, and her long, strong fingers as pliers to pull out our baby teeth.

She had five children of her own in her cramped council house in the Lost City estate in Tipton where we all lived. With fires to light and a range to black lead, plus chickens in the back yard and a husband who, by all accounts, had once left her to start another family with a woman in Shropshire, she had her hands full. In addition, her aged mother and dependant older sister both lived next door to her, with us.

The last thing Big Aunt Ginny needed was to have to take care of us while our mother went to work and our dad was in the hospital!

How long our dad was in the hospital for I didn't know, and I turned away to think about it while Aunt Ginny relentlessly scrubbed my brother's nose. Any minute now, she'd discover his first ever loose "tootsie peg" as she droolingly called them, and all hell would break loose!

I remembered being at Nan's, about two miles away, in Walker Street. While Dave and I played in the garden and Nan and Mom busied themselves in the small kitchen extension grandly called "the verandah", Dad roared off on his motor bike to go for a lunch time drink.

When he had the crash, they found a bag of sweets in his pocket and whenever I thought of them, I felt a rush of guilt. It must have been our fault, mine and Dave's, that the accident happened, because on his way back from the "Golden Cup" Dad had stopped to buy us dolly mixtures.

Anyway, there he was now, in Dudley Guest hospital, and we weren't allowed to see him. He had, as my Nan gravely told everybody, something called a "fractured femur." It sounded very grand and serious, and the impact of it had changed our lives.

Now, Mom went out to work, and because it was school holidays and Granny Coley and Aunt Maud were too old to take care of us, we had to spend our days with Big Aunt Ginny.

Gone were the delights of coming sleepily downstairs in the morning to cups of sweet, milky tea, and butter spread on soft white bread from the baker's man, and melted under the grill. Instead, we were bundled next door to share in a much less leisurely breakfast of puffed wheat, where there was never enough to go round, while Mom dashed off to catch her bus to the factory.

Gone too, was the prospect of going out to play in the street or the the outlying waste ground we called "the fields", because Big Aunt Ginny took her responsibilities seriously, and was full of warnings about the nearby "cut". We might be a nuisance, but she was determined to keep her eye on us!

"Car-rul!" As my brother escaped triumphantly from under her arm, his tooth miraculously undetected, Aunt Ginny looked round for her next victim. "Cum on, let's get that tidemark off yer neck!"

Panic stricken, I caught at my breath. Even though I no longer had any loose teeth for her to operate on, being in Aunt Ginny's grasp was still a fate worse than death.

Just as the big woman bore down on me, however, there came the sound of the side gate banging, and my eldest cousin, Brenda came in, tired and grimy, from the factory.

"Yer mother's comin'!" she said offhandedly in my direction, as she walked into the cluttered back kitchen, and without waiting for a reply: "Any tay in that pot, our Mother? I'm spittin' feathers!"

As Big Aunt Ginny turned to the gas stove and the perpetually stewing teapot, I took advantage of the moment to slip out of the door. Relief and excitement turmoiled inside me as I hurried in the twilight across Aunt Ginny's "fowd" past our kitchen window, and to the entry at the side of the house.

In this entry, my cousins and I put on plays and sang and "tap danced" through all the popular songs we heard on the wireless. We played two ball for hours against the side of the house, vying with each other to see how high we could bounce the balls. On bonfire night, we ran up and down the entry, clutching each other and screaming in terror when the big boys from next door threw bangers and jumping jacks at us from behind their shields of dustbin lids.

Now, as I stood at the top of the entry, my whole attention was focused on the figure that came through the opening in the square bricked council built wall. My mother was slim and graceful, with that lingering element of film star beauty that had been all the rage in the 1940s, a decade ago.

Her eyes were green, her hair, dark and wavy, hidden beneath the intricate folds of the turban which, along with the cross-over cotton pinafore beneath her coat, marked her out as a worker.

As she came towards me, half hidden in the shadows of the dying afternoon, it was as if the moment became suspended. My own bubble of fear and insecurity suddenly burst into the knowledge, too keep for works, that now she was here, everything would be all right. My brother and I were safe.

On her part, I sensed a surge of gratification and new energy as with an almost clumsy gesture, she pressed me to her side. Whatever demands and difficulties had made up her long day, work was over now, not only for the night, but right up until Monday morning.

Within a couple of hours, she'd be happily opening the lid of her new gramophone and putting on the one record that made up her collection. "Wilomenah is plump and round!" she'd sing almost mischievously as she caught up with the dusting, and we'd need no encouragement at all to join in as we danced around the kitchen.

"Where's our Dave?" she asked, and, looking up, I saw her face, all alight with smiling. I breathed in deeply, catching the sharp, unmistakable smell of factory slurry oil and with it, mingling strangely and yet so sweetly, the rare sharpness of fresh fruit. "I've brought yer some strawberries fer yer tay!"

CHAPTER
TWO

"Theer 'e is, look! Wave to yer dad!"

Obediently, I squinted up at the far away upstairs window, and waved my hand. Dudley Guest hospital seemed very big, and it felt strange not to be allowed to go inside.

Still, Nan had encouraged us on the bus, we COULD stand on the wall while she and Mom took it in turns to go in, and if we were really lucky, Dad would be able to see us. And wave.

"Where?" Dave's frustrated voice rose as he wobbled on tiptoe beside me. The wall was slippery, topped with iron railings and prickly bushes ran along its vast, impenetrable length, pushing into our legs. "I cor see him!"

"Can't." Nan corrected, automatically, and then, as a faint movement came at the window. "Theer, look! That's 'is arm — waving to yer both!"

I screwed up my eyes even further, trying to recognise the dismembered arm. But it had been so long now since Dad's accident that I sometimes wondered if I would recognise any of him, let alone a single arm.

"It'll be a long job," Nan told everyone who asked about him, and lots who didn't. "'E's bin fower months in the Guest, and soon, it's off to Patsull 'all for 'is convalescence . . .!"

The hand stopped waving, withdrawn as suddenly as it had appeared in the window frame, and Nan sighed. "Come on," she said, lifting us both from the wall. "Visiting's over now. Yer Mom'll be out soon."

On the way home on the bus, she suddenly opened her black handbag and took out a paper twist of sweets, chocolate drops encrusted with hundreds and thousands, crunchy and damply delicious against the tongue.

"Thanks, Nanna," I said, leaning back against her comfortable bulk, while Mom lifted Dave onto her knee.

Nan looked over my head, taking in Mom's quiet, pale face, distracted by the visit and solemnly lovely. "Dow thank me," she said, meaningfully, "Thank yer dad. 'E's the one who sent 'em for yer, out of the 'ospital — day 'e, Liza?"

As Mom nodded, surprise added sweetness to the unexpected treat in my mouth and relief lifted my spirits as I realised. Our dad must have forgiven us at last for causing him to crash his motor bike! The chocolate drops were a tangible sign of that — new sweets in return for the ones I never saw, that had been found in his jacket pocket on that day when everything had changed.

From then on, it seemed natural to link his hospital life with my own routine through the common denominator of food. "Me dad 'as this in the hospital,"

9

I'd say, as I unrolled and began to eat, lengthways, a slice of jammy swiss roll, only to be told sharply that my dad didn't eat it like THAT!

The day came for Dad to go to Patsull, an ancestral hall which had been turned into a convalescent home. Though only about ten miles away, on the other side of Wolverhampton, it might as well have been on the other side of the world.

As usual, all the information came through Nan, who told whoever was lisening that 'our "Arold" would be taken, along with his crutches, in the ambulance, early on the Saturday morning.

In the middle of Friday night, I was woken up by a sudden commotion from downstairs.

Creeping, shivering, onto the lino-covered landing, I peered through the bannisters at the scene below. Granny Coley and Aunt Maud were both snoring loudly in the bedroom next door, and I had left my brother, also sleeping soundly, in the feather bed we shared.

"Oo is it?" Mom's astonished figure nervously opened the front door to the tall, awkwardly determined man on crutches. The blast of cold darkness from outside filled with Mom's remonstrations and Dad's sketchy but bold description of his escape from Dudley Guest as he fell into her arms.

Mom sighed and shook her head as he told of stealing a coat from a lobby cupboard and sneaking out in it after Sister had done her late night ward round. By the time he got to the part about hobbling through the dark streets and along the cut towpath, his voice carrying through the house, my brother and I were both at his knee, listening, wide eyed with wonder and admiration.

"Well, it's too lert ter goo back now," Mom said, as we bore our hero towards the kitchen. "Berra mek some cocoa."

Next morning, there came a fierce banging at the front door, and unknown disapproving male voices in the hall. Dave and I had just been getting used to having Dad around again, a muscular figure whose crutches seemed to fill the small living room, and who had so many interesting stories to tell. Now, the men in the ambulance had come to take him away again.

"You might think you've got away with it, my lad," said the older man, as he stood by the open door. "but if anything comes of this escapade the doctors would be within their rights not to treat you!"

Whatever that meant, it was obvious to me. As he winked his eye, picked up his crutches, and prepared to go to Patsull, our Dad was just glad to have been home to see us all!

CHAPTER
THREE

It was while dad was away at Patsull that Mrs. Miller put her head in the gas oven. The whisper went round the streets and finally caught up with us kids, playing in the disused Anderson shelter at the bottom of our garden.

"Why did 'er do that?" I asked my cousin Eva and was told with a knowing look it was because Mrs Miller was having another babby.

"This one'll mek thirteen," Eva said, casually pulling a peach she had stolen from Jimmy Tarr's fruit shop from the leg of her navy blue knickers. "Want a bite o' this?"

I hastily shook my head, digging my toe in the dirt floor of the tin shelter as I thought about Mrs. Miller's dilemma. How must it have felt, to put your head in the gas oven and wait to die? I couldn't imagine it, and it was too deep and scarey to try for long.

In the house, Mom was talking about it as she poured Granny Coley's tea. "Gud job Mrs. Grainger come to the back door an' smelt the gas, Gran," she said, as the old lady nodded from her place by the fire. 'er threatened it this time last year, if yo remember, when her got catched wi' young Pearl."

"Ar, the poor wench'll 'ave one on every quarry tile afore E'S finished with 'er!" Granny Coley prophesied as she pulled her shawl more closely round her ninety-year old shoulders, and meaningfully sniffed. We all thought silently about Mr Miller — a weaselly looking man who went past to the pub every Friday night.

Suddenly noticing me in the doorway, she pushed out a boney hand. "C'mere, cock. Let's see if I've gorra copper fer yer!"

Mom tutted her disapproval, but Granny ignored her. Opening her worn flap-over purse, a coin for myself and my brother. "Ere, 'ave this penny apiece. Goo and get some suck!"

Clutching the big, brown pennies, we hurried up the road to the sweet shop kept by Jimmy Tarr's brother, Sid. There it was possible to buy two "hard juice" licorice sticks, a paper full of "kali" powder, or an everlasting strip for a penny.

"I'll 'ave an everlasting strip," I told Dave decisively. "They last forever!" As we later walked home, I sucked thoughtfully at the thin toffee bar, filled as usual with the hope the magical name always gave me.

The sweet was just breaking, as usual, into disappearing bits as we turned back into West Road. The Miller family lived on the corner, separated from our house by broken palings and a patch of dirt. Hanging around the side of the house were children of all ages and both sexes while others played in the uncultivated back garden.

The youngest but two, a white-haired toddler called Sheila, sat on the ground eating dirt off a broken teaspoon. She was wearing a torn and filthy pink cotton dress and her legs and feet were bare.

Thinking of her mother and the gas oven, I stopped and broke off a big piece of the everlasting strip, now looking decidedly worse for wear. 'Ere yow am, Sheila" I said, holding it by the palings.

Like a shot, Sheila dropped the spoon and came towards me, her mouth and hands streaked with the blackness of the earth. She didn't say thank you, but just the look on her face made the sacrafice complete.

When we got back into the house, it was obvious that Mom and Granny Coley had had "words." "Words" were what I often overheard from Granny and Aunt Maud's bedroom when, late at night, the two old ladies sat up in their feather bed and hissed and disagreed with each other about the treatment they were receiving at the hands of my mother.

"Er as we pension, yow' know, Our Mother! Ever'y penny goos into 'er puss, when 'er's bin to the post office!"

"Dow be ser saft, Maud! Er's runnin' the 'wum, ay 'er? An' now 'Arold's away, laid up in the 'ospital, 'er's got 'er work cut out!"

Now, the "words" had been serious enough to set Granny Coley's mouth in a thin, tight line, while Mom's face was white and her green eyes bright with unshed tears. In her hands, she held the copy of "Wilomenah" in its brown paper sleeve.

"Ar, the gramaphone's gone!" she intercepted as Dave and I both stared in amazement at the empty patch of lino on which had stood her pride and joy. "They've bin an' fetched it back cos I got behind with the payments!"

"PAYMENTS !" Granny Coley muttered. "Shouldn't 'ave 'ad it if yow couldn't afford it! — Never bin so ashamed as when that van come to the door — an' all the neighbours gawpin' — knowin' we business!"

That evening, to make matters worse, the last penny ran out in the electric light meter. As we were plunged into darkness, Mom jumped to her feet and hurried into the brick coal hole, which led directly off the kitchen.

"We'll build up the fire wi' slack an' find out all the candles," she said. "Now stop schraaching, yow two — and dow worry, Gran. We'll soon 'ave some light again."

Before long, she had banked up the fire and filled the kettle at the kitchen sink, ready for the long business of making tea which I knew would taste all smokey from the black-leaded grate. Deftly lighting candle stubs, she let a drop of wax fall into the saucers and tin lids which were our candlesticks.

The small room was filled with a strange and silent glow and I watched, as if suspended, the shadow of Granny Coley, hunched and immobile in her armchair, growing vast and travelling up the wall and across the ceiling. As usual, my brother started to try to make the shadows of birds and animals with his fingers, while from the table the usually silent Aunt Maud began to

15

describe how, in the days before electricity, she used to make the white cotton covers for gas mantles.

"I crotcheted 'em, see," she pushed gnarled hands into the shadowy room. "When I got back from the glass works, y'know!"

"Yes, Aunt Maud." I nodded, remembering what I'd overheard about the old lady's habits of forgetfulness. My mother was always complaining that she took food, usually fruit she had bought from Jimmy Tarr's, and hid it in the bedroom, meaning to eat it but always forgetting, so that its rich, rancid smell would eventually fill the house.

But we loved her stories about the canalside glassworks where she had worked for forty years, especially the vivid descriptions of the glass blowers making the lampshades that were designed to hang from chains in people's living rooms.

"They use a big, long pipe — wi' a little blob o' glass on the end," Aunt Maud said now, her thin face beneath the cap of white hair growing animated in the candlelight. "Real bobby dazzlers they mek, all outa that little blob! An' at the finish, they all come to me to be washed all clean an' bright in me big sink afore they got packed!"

How many lampshades would Aunt Maud have washed in forty years, I wondered idly before realising it sounded like a sum we might be given at school. Glancing at my mother's tired face, I realised she would soon be packing my brother and me off to bed, cocoa-less and without the comforting accompaniment of either radio or radiogram from downstairs.

"Tell we another story, Aunt Maud," I begged, as the broken candles began to go out and the fire spluttered under the weight of the blackened kettle. "Tell we about when you went 'op-pickin'!" Scooting across the floor on my bottom, I settled against her legs, reluctant to ever be moved.

CHAPTER
FOUR

"Hands on heads!" At the signal from Mrs Whitecraft, we all sat to attention in the narrow desks at St Mark's C. of E Junior School, Spring Street. From my seat at the dunces' end of the class, I saw the headmaster, Mr Lodge, coming along the corridor with two other figures I vaguelly recognised from West Road.

As they entered the classroom, propelled by a push from Mr Lodge, I saw to my horror that their heads were shaved and covered in sores which had been painted in purple gentian, the tell tale signs of the infectious skin complaint, impetigo.

"I want you all to take a look at these two individuals and learn a lesson from them, best beloved!" the headmaster boomed, as the boys shuffled their feet and stared fixedly at the floor. "Mrs Whitecraft and I both know where they come from!" He exchanged a meaningful nod with the stiff-backed teacher. "And we both know where they will end up — as road sweepers, or worse, in prison! Shun them and their impetigo, best beloved, and make sure you never become dirty and low like them!"

As the boys were taken to be exhibited to the class beyond the school's sliding partition, I wondered why their mother had sent them to school with the impetigo. When Dave and I had picked it up from a playmate last year, we were kept away — wearing hats and walking to the park, scurrying with our mother past the noise of the school playground. Impetigo had been a scourge, like nits, and certainly not something to be put on display.

"Hands off heads! Time for tables!" As Mrs Whitecraft gave the usual command, I held my breath, half heartedly joining in the chorus of the hated multiplication tables, and hoping against hope I wouldn't be called upon to do a sum on my own.

My thoughts were still on Mr Lodge's visit and his scathing words about where the shaven headed boys came from. North, South, East and West roads were all part of the "Lost City" slum clearance area of council houses.

It was a place cut off by canal banks and further isolated by the local electricity station, with its dank and ugly cooling towers. Inhabited by rag and bone men whose horses and carts were interspersed with the odd abandoned car, its few streets seemed to hold most of the largest and all of the toughest families in Tipton.

I knew without even looking round me that all the kids who sat at the dunces' end of Mrs Whitecraft's class came, like me, from the Lost City. And it was then, remembering what Mr Lodge had said about road sweepers and prisons, that I decided that I wasn't going to stay on the dunces' side any longer!

At the exact opposite of the class, the two seats nearest the window were always occupied by Mary Gregory and her friend, Pamela Simms. These two godlike creatures were, to my eyes, on a plane apart. Not only did they answer all the questions Mrs Whitecraft could throw their way, they were smartly dressed, had parents who took them to church, and possessed all the pens, books and pencil crayons they could possibly need for school work.

It was a foregone conclusion that every week when we had our "class test", it would be Mary and Pamela who would get most marks and vie for top place. Until now!

As I bent over the paper that Thursday afternoon, I felt my breath quicken. Suddenly, I just knew I could do this. It was as if I'd just woken up from a long sleep, especially when I saw this week's test was all about writing a story based on a book we had recently read.

My book collection, like my mother's record collection, comprised of only one. I had read and re-read *Little Women* endless times since Nan gave it to me for my birthday, and soon I lost myself in the world of Meg, Jo, Beth and Amy.

Next day, when Mrs. Whitecraft came into the class room, she seemed somewhat subdued. Unlike most weeks, she did not hurry with the test results, beaming on her star pupils as she handed out their accolades. Instead, she shuffled the papers and sat at her big desk, looking uncertain and embarrassed.

Finally, she got up and began to give the papers back, starting as usual with the dunces' side, building up the excitement for the successful ones who deserved to savour it. My mouth went dry as I realised mine wasn't coming back, and moreover, that Mrs Whitcroft was avoiding looking in my direction at all!

With a sigh, she walked to the top of the class and wordlessly handed Mary and Pamela their papers. I saw them exchange a surprised look as she went back and sat down again, one paper still in her hand. But held near the corner, almost as if she was afraid she would catch something from it.

"Er, this week there has been quite a surprise," she began, clearing her throat, and still not looking at me. "The highest mark in the test has been achieved by Carol Sheldon. Well done, Carol."

In the stunned silence that followed, I felt my heart leap in both delight and terror. Delight because I had done it, terror at the magnitude of what I had actually done. How was I going to get on, sitting with Mary Gregory and Carol Simms, with their spotless dresses and acceptable ways? I didn't even have a pencil case to take to the top desk, so bathed in sunlight from the great sash window. How could I do the school work without the equipment I knew my family couldn't afford to provide?

Mrs Whitecraft cleared her throat, her stern face darkening with colour as, trembling with anticipation and pride, I began to get to my feet. Quickly, she held out a restraining hand more forbidding than any five barred gate.

"It's all right, Carol," she said, quickly, "You can stay where you are. This week's test was just a practice."

CHAPTER
FIVE

Dad was home at last, brought back from Patsull late one Friday afternoon in the same ambulance that had taken him away. The ambulance was immediately mobbed with excited and curious children so that I had trouble getting near the figure in crutches that emerged.

"Dad! Dad!" I finally pushed through to his side, and he reached down to awkwardly ruffle my hair.

"Yow've sprung up," he commented, and then, setting his face forward, he began to make his way on the crutches through the gate and up to the front door, where Mom was waiting, Dave fidgeting excitedly at her side.

"Lift me up! I cor see!"

Once in the house, Dad was given the place of honour on the couch in the scarcely used front room, where a fire had been lit to welcome him. The furniture gleamed, the space where the gramophone had been filled by Granny Coley's big old-fashioned sideboard.

While Aunt Maud went to put the kettle on, Mom took her place almost shyly at Dad's side while Dave and I sat on the floor.

"Well, this is a bit different to Patsull 'all," Dad grinned, as he eased his leg along the horsehair couch. He began to describe the convalescent hospital, and within seconds, I could see the upstairs wards with the smart and busy nurses, and the long, sweeping staircase, in my mind's eye.

"Guess wot, our Carol? We 'ad a visit from Queen Mary last wick!" he went on, obviously enjoying the way my mouth dropped open in awe. "All the poor buggers in the upstairs wards struggled along the landing and down the stairs, nearly breakin' their necks to get outside to see 'er! Some of em couldn't 'obble more than a few steps. In the end, there was on'y me still left in bed!"

"Day YOW want to see Queen Mary then, our 'arold?" I realised that while he'd been speaking, Nan had arrived, her shopping bag full of goodies for the invalid.

Grinning, Dad reached out for a grape and polished it on his sleeve before popping it into my brother's mouth. "That's what the matron asked me," he replied, "But I tode 'er straight. If Queen Mary wants to see me — let 'er come up 'ere!"

The next afternoon, in the Anderson shelter, I recounted the story to Big Aunt Ginny's children. Though I didn't really understand it, I sensed it made my dad a hero, of sorts, someone who made up his own mind about things.

Now he was back, everything would be all right, I told myself. Mom would be able to stay at home again, and there would be no more need for Dave and I to go to Aunt Ginny's.

On Monday afternoon, I walked home with Eva and her sister Rose as always, collecting Dave from the infants on the way. Mrs. Whitecraft had been unusually encouraging, giving me nine out of ten for my English composition.

But I no longer aspired to sit at the top of the class. My dreams had taken a different turn, and it was all thanks to Carroll Levis and his radio "Discoveries."

"Did yow 'ear 'im on the wireless yesterday?" I asked my companions enthusiastically. Just the memory of the entertainer's warm, drawling voice — the knowledge that we shared the same Christian name — was enough to make me want to dance through the whole "Lost City".

"This wench was on — 'on'y six, an' 'er sung, just like we do in the entry!"

In my fruitful imagination, the girl had been wearing a red satin skirt, just like the one Nan had promised to make me one day. A skirt which whirled and sparkled, as it danced along with you.

"If I give my heart to yoooooo!" I warbled, off key, as we at last reached the entry which was our theatre. "Will you promise to be troooo! Now my dad's 'um, I'm goin' to ask 'im to write to Carrol Levis and get me on the wireless! After all, 'e nearly met Queen Mary!"

CHAPTER
SIX

"They've set somebody else on while I've bin in the 'ospital!" All my dreams of fame and fortune crashed around me as I overheard my parents' conversation.

Dad had come in late for his tea and I could tell from the smell on his breath that he'd called in at the "Golden Cup".

Washed out from her day at the factory, Mom snapped back at him, "Yow said they'd keep your job open! What'll we do now?"

She looked around her as if trapped, and for some reason I suddenly remembered the stories she'd told me about her own mother dying when she was just a baby and her father running off with somebody else. She was an orphan, and the thought of that always made me sad and shivery.

"Well, it ay my fault they've done the dirty on me!" Dad's blue eyes flashed and he snatched up the coat he had just taken off. He too looked around, at the two old ladies whose disapproving silence filled the poky living room, my brother, just starting to grizzle for his tea, me, horrified, swallowing every word and gesture whole.

"Ar'm off out!" he announced, and a moment later, the back door slammed.

"Good riddance!" Mom spat the words between gritted teeth before launching into a turmoil of frenzied activity. Within minutes, the fire was made up and a meal of baked beans, fried eggs and bacon set out on the table.

Chairs were silently pulled out and cups of tea made and poured from the brown earthenware pot.

"Dow worry, my wench," Granny Coley said, as she came across from the fireside with her stick in hand.

"Ar, Liza. E'll be back." Aunt Maud put in knowingly, "An' e'll soon get another job, p'raps even at the glassworks!"

Mom, busy cutting bread from the thick white loaf, merely nodded. Her green eyes were both sad and angry, and I sighed as I climbed onto my chair. Even though it wasn't Friday, our traditional bath night, I had a feeling my brother and I would be scrubbed from head to toe in the tin bath on the hearth tonight. Packed off to bed while it was still light, I knew I'd lie there long after Dave was asleep, my head still tingling from the onslaught with the steel nit comb, my stomach rumbling because of the obligatory dose of Syrup of Figs.

Aunt Maud's prophetic words came true a few days later. Dad did get a new job. But it wasn't at the canalside glassworks. It was at the Austin car factory, far away in Birmingham!

"It's awl right for some! 'E'll be on twenty quid a wick now!" I heard Aunt Ginny say to one of the neighbours, as she pegged out her washing in the back yard. "I s'pose it'll be all swank, then, with no thoughts of them that's looked after the bloody kids fer nothin!"

As she nodded in our direction, I took a deep breath. With no loose teeth in my head, and the prospect of freedom in view, I suddenly found the courage to blurt out:

"Why dow yow like we, Aunt Ginny? What've we done?"

Big Aunt Ginny's mouth dropped open, despatching the clothes pegs she'd been holding in it swiftly to the muddy path. Stepping back, she glared down at me from a great height, angry colour mounting her gaunt face.

"Oo'd yer think YO am, questionin' me, yer cheeky little bugger!" she burst out, spittle flying, as she seized and shook me. "After all I've done for yer, and yo on'y a pack o — of bloody lodgers!"

She ranted on, finally dragging both Dave and myself away from the gawping neighbour and into the steamy back kitchen and the other children.

As Aunt Ginny turned to the wooden dolly tub and lifted the clothes posher, I had two very different thoughts going through my head at the same time.

The first was, I was glad I wasn't one of those cotton shirts Aunt Ginny was bashing in the hot water and suds. The second was, I had to find out what "lodgers" meant!

CHAPTER
SEVEN

"We'm goin' to decorate!" Mom announced the Saturday after Dad's first pay packet. She had a scarf on her head and her floral pinafore was fastened tightly around her middle. "So yow two goo out to play!"

Dave had been interestedly stirring the bucket of "whitewash" set carefully on the kitchen floor. "Yeller, it's all yeller!" he exclaimed.

Nan, who had arrived to help, began to bundle us into our coats. "It's ter do lemons," she said, and as I frowned. "Yow'll see, when it's finished. Now, gerrout from under we feet!"

I was only too glad to get out, hating the way the furniture had to be covered in old sheets and the curtains taken down from the front room window. It made everything seem so unfamiliar.

Aunt Maud and Granny Coley were the lucky ones, I thought as I led my brother through the back door onto the yard. They'd been allowed to stay in bed until all the disruption was over!

When I looked into the Anderson shelter, Eva was sitting on her coat, industriously corking, thin, nail-bitten fingers flying as she passed the blue wool between the nails hammered into an old cotton reel.

"Shut the door, quick!" she hissed. "I'm 'iding from our mother, mekking a pair of slippers!"

Only too glad of the invitation, I shoved Dave in the general direction of a group of marbles-playing lads and went inside. Sitting down by Eva, the ridged sides of the shelter against my back, I watched her pull the short piece of knitting through the reel before asking the question, "Ev. Yowr muther said we was on'y lodgers. What does it mean?"

Eva looked down on me from the height and experience of her twelve years. "It means it ay yowr 'ouse!" she said, pointedly. "It's Granny's name in the rent book, not yer dad's — so er could mek yer leave any time 'er wanted!"

Make us leave? I couldn't believe it, and I frowned at Eva uncomprehendingly. Vaguelly, I understood that Granny Coley and Aunt Maud had lived together in an old house in Horseley Heath that had been pulled down before Mom and Dad got married. But 3 West Road was the only place I knew as home. I couldn't imagine being anywhere else.

Realising Eva was looking almost as triumphant as Big Aunt Ginny had, I jumped to my feet. "It dow bother me!" I said with a confidence I certainly didn't feel. "If I had ter leave, I'd goo an' live in a caravan like the gypos over the fields! That'd be really good!"

Later, hoping for a word with my mother, I sneaked back house through the open front door to find the house totally transformed! The front room walls, ceiling and paintwork were all covered with an uneven pattern of yellow blobs that even included the floor to ceiling cupboards.

"Like it?" beamed Mom, her face smudged beneath the loosened scarf. "We dun it with sponges. It's all the rage, yer Nan says!"

"Ar, that's right, Lize, all the nobs've 'ad it dun!" Nan looked pinker and more exhilarated that I'd ever seen her. As the door creaked open and the two old ladies came suspiciously from upstairs, she called cheerily,

"That's it, Sarah. Come on in — yow an' all, Maud! Come and see what a difference a few lemons mek!"

"Thuz a lot of lemons!" My brother, tiring of marbles, appeared at my side, pointing in the direction of the living room.

"We 'ad some of the stuff left over." The two painters looked at each other as the gasps of Granny and Maud carried back to them. "So we thought we'd do in the scullery an' all!"

"Wot the bloody 'ell's THIS!" The back door banged and Dad's raised, astonished voice was suddenly filling the place. He stormed in, eyes blazing, as he took in the continuing blobs which seemed to reach as far as the eye could see.

Like two guilty schoolgirls, the besmirched decorators stood in silence unable, it seemed, to look at him, no longer wanting to look at one another.

"It's lemons, 'Arold," Nan said, unneccessarily. Suddenly, a wide smile broke across her face and a moment later, her shoulders started shaking with suppressed laughter.

"Ooo-er!" Irresistibly, Mom caught the giggle. As she looked again at the result of her day's labour, her hand was clasped across her mouth. "D-dun yer think we've gorra bit carried away, cock?" she asked, rhetorically.

"Carried away?" Dad rolled up his sleeves and picked up the empty bucket. "I should think the two on yers 'ad spots in front of yer eyes!"

He marched into the kitchen and a moment later came back, with the bucket filled to the brim with water. "Waesh 'em off!" he ordered as Mum and Nan both stared at him aghast. "I mean it, Liza! Ar'm gooin' ter bed, and when I get up, I dow want to see even one lemon in either of these rooms!"

"S'pose we'll arrer do it!" There was no sign of Mom's earlier enthusiasm as she sighed and went into the kitchen for some cleaning rags. "Come on, kids, yow c'n 'elp me an' yer Nan waesh it off!"

While Granny Coley kept up a running commentary for the benefit of Aunt Maud, I stood by Nan, dipped a cloth in the cold water and experimentally wiped at one of the lower smudges. As it spread and ran and gradually disappeared, I thought it was a shame we couldn't keep at least a few of the lemons. For a while, they had made everything look different.

CHAPTER
EIGHT

"I'm askin' yer to LEAVE, Liza!" At first, I thought the urgently whispered words were part of my dream and I struggled to breathe in the dark, airless room. Then I realised the voice was coming, not from Granny Coley's room, but from where my parents slept, on the other side of the narrow landing. And it was Dad who was speaking!

Carefully not to wake my brother, I pushed off the heavy greeen eiderdown and lowered my bare feet to the cold lino. It seemed miles to the door, past the huge, oppressive dressing table with its three mirrors, and the wardrobe which made it almost impossible to walk at the bottom of the bed.

The bedroom door was slightly ajar, and I prised it open further as I slipped through it. I stood, shivering in my thin pyjamas, as the icyness of the house seemed to descend damply over me.

Over the familiar sounds of Granny and Aunt Maud's night noises, I caught my mother's heartfelt sigh, followed by her whispered reply, "Oh, 'Arold, I've told yer till I'm sick, I cor leave Gran. I promised I'd tek care on 'er fer as long as 'er needs me!"

Kneeling on the floor, I listened to Dad's unhappy voice, trying to persaude her to move away from 3 West Road, and her agitated but still decisive reply, "Gran took me in when I had nowheer ter goo. 'Er went out scrubbin' floors at the age of 70 because my own ferther was gonna 'ave me put in the workuss!" she reminded him. "When the council gid 'er this 'ouse, 'er begged me not to leave her!"

"Even though that means we'll never 'ave a plairce of we own? Yow, me and the kids?" Dad's reply was almost lost in the rumble of snores from the room next door, but I still caught the longing and the supressed anger of his tone.

Next day, when I got up for school, he had already gone to work, and Mom, pale faced but busier than ever, was sorting out the washing. "I want yow ter goo to the butchers on yowr way 'um, Carol," she said, picking up an old envelope and a stub of pencil. "Gerra quarter o' sausage and two rashers o' Cumberland baercon fer yer dad's tay."

"Aw — do I 'ave to?" After my disturbed night, the last thing I needed was a trek to the shop which, contrary to being "on my way home" was actually nearly a mile in the opposite direction.

To my hurt surprise, Mom jabbed at me with the reddened hand she had been using to drop the clothes into the steaming dolly tub. Her green eyes flashed and I stepped instinctively backwards out of her reach.

"Ar, yow bloody well do!" she burst out, distractedly pushing a slice of bread and melted butter into my brother's hand. "I wo 'ave time with all this waeshin' ter do! So gerroff ter school and do as yow'm tode!"

On the way home from the butchers, I stopped near the cooling towers and carefully undid the white wrapped parcel. Squeezing a small, pink lump of meat from the one of one of the two sausages, I put it into my mouth and slowly savoured it as I made my suddenly reluctant way home.

I didn't overhear any more talk about us leaving West Road. But over the next few months, Dad became a shadowy figure Dave and I scarcely ever saw. Busy with concerts in the entry and struggles at school, I hardly missed him, though it was obvious from her white face and pinched lips that Mom did, very much.

Her unhappiness made her short tempered and we learnt to keep out of her way, especially when she was banging round in the coalshed, or furiously cleaning the windows with vinegar water and scrunched up newspaper.

Big Aunt Ginny no longer featured so largely in our lives, in fact she acknowledged me with only a disapproving sniff since my outburst in the back garden. As the seasons slipped by, and our street games went, unspokenly, from skipping ropes to hide and seek and back again, I began to long, like my father, for change and adventure in my life.

The only place it seemed to be available was in the pages of books, and in my imagination, I spent hours with Jo, Meg, Beth and Amy March, whose "Marmee" was at once too nice and wholly desirable.

Unnoticed by Mrs Whitecraft, I read everthing I could take from the classroom book cupboard, from *Peter Rabbit*, to *Pilgrim's Progress*.

Then Eva took me, early one Monday evening, to the public library in Toll End Road, an old, single storey building with wide steps leading up to revolving glass doors. And I fell through — like Alice — into another dimension.

"Come ON!" hissed Eva, wiping her hands on her cotton skirt as she led me up to the polished desk. "This is wheer we JOIN!"

Mesmerised, I was still staring round, trying to take in the wonderful, amazing sight and smell of so many books — thousands and thousands of them — on shelves all around the walls.

"Yes? What do you want?" The bespectacled librarian seemed very old and stern, twice as formidable, if that were possible, as our school teachers. She peered from below her "Silence" notice as if we were some lower form of life. Disgust and suspicion filled her narrow face as Eva, sniffing noisily, said we wanted to "join."

"You won't be able to take out any books today!" Although she didn't say it, I knew she had seen the tell tale "Lost City" stamp on our foreheads, and was propelling us towards the dunces' part of her library.

She explained about the important green card that had to be filled in and signed by somebody called a rate payer, and when all that had been done, we would have to pay a penny joining fee.

"Oh." Eva's face fell at the enormity of it all. But as I took my green card and prepared to carry it carefully away, I was already working it out. Just how I could get that penny.

CHAPTER
NINE

Dad was in the entry with Eileen Dawson when I got
back from Nan's. I was a bit surprised because Eileen
was "common". She worked at the transport café, wore
bright red lipstick and smoked cigarettes in the street.
I'd heard the grown ups discussing what they called her
"goings on" very often, though I never seemed quick
enough to catch the precise, mysterious details.

"So long, then," Dad straightened up from where he
seemed to have been standing quite close to Eileen. She
patted her hair and smiled before teetering away on
high heels.

"Ta ra then, 'Al," she called over her shoulder, her
voice sounding low and almost challenging. I frowned,
not only at her tone, but at the shortening of his name,
but he didn't seem to notice its strangeness.

"An what yow bin up to, our Carol?" he asked,
leading me companionably towards the back door. I
needed no second bidding to describe how Nan had
agreed to sign my green card, and, more to the point,
give me the penny I needed to join the library. A warm
glow seemed to spread inside me as I remembered how
Nan had listened, sitting side by side with me on the
sofa.

"I dow own me own 'ouse, so I dow know if I AM a ratepayer!" she'd admitted finally, biting her lip as she read through the card again. "P'raps I'll get into trouble for signin' this?"

Then, she'd looked at my crestfallen face, and hers had softened. "Giz it 'ere. Yow'm wuth any trouble, an' I'll gi' yer the penny wi' pleasure!"

The next night, I sat by the fire reading my first library book, while Mom made a rag rug for the hearth. I knew it was for Christmas which would, so Nan said, be better than we'd hoped this year, now Dad had his job at the Austin factory.

The rug was to be a mixture of black, red and green, all strips cut up from clothes too old to be even given to the rag and bone man. Mom had bought a sack and cut it open and washed it before taking her "podger" — a sharpened clothes peg — and pushing the strips of cloth through.

"I'd goo mad if I day ave this ter do," she said suddenly, simply, addressing me as if I were an adult. I nodded, knowing her despair had something to do with the way Dad had got changed into his best shirt and gone out, as she was helping Granny and Aunt Maud to bed.

Long after the lights were out, I lay in bed waiting for the sounds of my father coming home, but I must have fallen asleep because I never heard him return to the house, and he'd gone off to catch the works coach to Birmingham before we got up for school.

Two days later, on Saturday, Aunt Maud took us to buy our Christmas presents. Every year, a little procession, comprising Dave and myself and Aunt Ginny's three youngest accompanied her to the toy shop near the glass-works at Dudley Port.

As we walked, Aunt Maud's white head bobbed. "I used to work at them glass works, yer know . . ."

I smiled as I fell into step with Eva and Rose, anticipating the shop, stacked from floor to ceiling with toys. The more expensive ones, the baby dolls with closing eyes and plastic shoes, and the bright realistic train sets with their metal tracks, were well out of our range. But Aunt Maud, despite her absentmindedness, never forgot what she COULD afford.

"Toy suck shaps, skippin' ropes." As she entered the shop like a ship in full sail with the crowd of us in her billowing sails, she glanced from Rose to her brother Joey and at his side, a saucer-eyed Dave. "An' let's see some dinky cars an' tool kits fer these lads!"

The shop keeper was tall and thin and wore a brown overall. I could tell the way he gulped and glanced at his watch that he remembered us from last year. "Yes, missis." With one eye on Aunt Maud's closely clutched purse and the other on Eva, who had wandered away to where an array of plastic dolls were stacked, he struggled to stay in control. "Toy sweet shops? We've had some new ones in for this Christmas with their own weighin' scales."

He put the box on the glass-fronted counter, and I caught a glimpse of the miniature sweet jars, the tiny plastic bags, and cardboard money and the pink scales, all displayed against a brightly coloured "sweet shop" background.

"C'n I 'ave one, Auntie Maud?" Rose asked eagerly, tugging at our great aunt's voluminous skirt. I knew she was anticipating the joys of selling the tiny dolly mixtures and fruit jellies, and could almost taste them on my own tongue.

"That's one settled, then!" Aunt Maud's false teeth flashed a smile at the visibly relieved shopkeeper. "Now wot about yow other wenches — dun yer want the serm?"

Eva and I looked at each other, both certain of what we didn't want. "A knittin' set, please," Eva said, pointing to a busy looking box just behind the shop keeper's head.

While it was reached down, and placed on the counter with Rose's sweetshop, I felt everyone's eyes on me.

"'Urry up, our Carol," my brother urged, eager to choose his dinky car. With six-year old wisdom, he looked up at his mate, our cousin, Joey "Bet er dow know what her wants," he wagered.

That was where he was quite wrong. Ever since we'd come into the Aladdin's cave of the shop, there had been only one treasure I'd had my heart set on.

"A writin' set," I burst out eagerly, pointing to the cream and gold box in the very corner of the counter display. "Wi' paerper an' env'lopes, an' all them little stamps!"

CHAPTER
TEN

"Dow cry, Dave!" Torn between embarrassment and sympathy, I handed my sobbing brother the bit of torn sheeting that served as my hankie. All the other kids who were spilling out of Ocker Hill infants to be met by their mothers seemed to be staring. And listening as my brother noisily broke his heart about not having a school Christmas party.

"Yow'm too big, now — that's just for the babbies' class!" I tried to make it sound encouraging. But I couldn't help feeling cheated on his behalf as I realised just how much he had been looking forward to a repeat of last year's end of term party.

"We'll have we own party on Saturday," I promised, hurrying him away from the prying eyes of our cousins and the ever present group of curious Miller children who followed raggedly after them. "A proper feast wi' oranges an, pop from Nan's, an' — an' fruit gums!"

Dave gave me back my hankie and wiped his nose on his sleeve. "C'n I ave the black uns?" he asked, craftily. "All the black uns?"

I looked back at the new infants with their clutched parcels and jelly streaked faces. "Oh, aw right," I acquieced, knowing even then I'd live to regret my generosity.

At home, we found to our surprise that Dad was home early, the car factory having finished for the Christmas break. Mom was busy frying bacon for our tea, and there was a great big smile on her face.

"Goo 'n' see wot yer dad's brought me fer Christmas!" she greeted. "It's in the front room, in the bay winder!"

Curiously, we hurried into the "best" room, to find Granny Coley huddled in her shawl by the unlit fire. "Dog!" she sniffed, nodding her head. "Theer — look — waerstin' good money on trankelments!"

I glanced warily back towards the living room while Dave dashed to the window ledge. "Cor, look at this!" he breathed, all his earlier upset forgotton.

I stood by his side, breathing deeply as I stared at the big statue, an Alsatian dog made out of chalk, with realistic markings and a red, open mouth, complete with painted teeth. The front paws were crossed, and the long tail curled round on the imitation grass base.

"It's BEAUTIFUL!" I sighed, ignoring Granny's second sniff. As I ran back in the direction of the tantalising bacon smell, I understood perfectly why Mom loved the dog so much. Not only did it add style to the room she spend so much time keeping spotless, but it was a present from Dad. Showing her, and everyone else, how much he loved her!

Christmas, I felt sure, was going to be better than ever this year, and it started next day, Christmas Eve, when all four of us walked to Great Bridge to do the shopping.

The cold air seemed to crackle with expectancy around the market and the shops, and people called out greetings to each other as they hurried busily along.

"Fust we get the bird, then the Christmas tree," Mum seemed to have the special shopping list in her head and for once, Dad was happy to take part, moving the feathered chicken from one arm to the other as he prepared to lift the small, spindly tree over his shoulder.

Nuts, tangerines, dates and figs were all bought at Adams huge fruit and vegetable shop, along with the potatoes, carrots and brussel sprouts which would help fill our plates on Christmas day.

We were just waiting for Mom to come out of Firkins cake shop with the Christmas pudding when a voice called. "'Arold! I thought it was yow!"

The familiar figure of Nan hurried over to us. "Good job it's on'y once a year!" she said, typically. "I've left yer grandad pluckin' the turkey!"

Before disappearing in the direction of the market, she reminded Dave and myself. "I'll see yow kids in the mornin'. Arn gorra surprise fer both of yer!"

"A red satin skirt! That's what MY surprise'll be!" I grandly told my cousins that afternoon when, banished by the busy grown ups, we crowded into the damp and chilly shelter. "My Nan said 'er'd mek me one aerges agoo!"

Eva glanced at me and I caught the unmistakable gleam of envy in her eyes before she stuck her thin nose into the cold air and said: "Well, WE'M 'avin' sucklin' pig fer dinner — me Dad's gone to the country to fetch it! An' our muther says a full bally c'n allus loff at fine clooz!"

A full belly AND fine clothes. Next day, I experienced the good fortune of having both. It didn't matter that Dad, after taking us to our grandparents, went off to the pub and made us late getting home for dinner. The dinner was waiting, with Granny and Aunt Maud at the table, proudly wearing under their long skirts, the knitted garters I'd made them for Christmas.

There was home-made ginger beer to wash down a chicken that had been cooked to perfection. And Mom smiled, her face shining with happiness, as she carefully poured a thimbleful of medicinal brandy onto the pudding and carried it, wreathed in blue flames, to the table. "Ready! Deep breath — now — all mek a wish!"

The satin skirt was a full circle of breathtaking scarlet. While my brother played with his surprise — an old wind-up gramophone with Woolworths cowboys and indians glued round the rim, I whirled and stamped. And dreamt to my heart's delight.

CHAPTER
ELEVEN

Going to fetch the coal was the worst errand in the world, and I was really glad I didn't have to do it on my own. Between them, Aunt Ginny and Mom had worked out a system whereby they shared the cost of a pram load and also got free child labour for the day.

"It's miles away!" I complained as my cousins waited in the entry with the huge battered pram with its high wheels and broken hood. "An' it's all uphill!"

"Dow be so saft, Carol. The wharf's on'y in New Road!" Since Christmas, Mom had seemed busier, and sharper than ever, her face growing more grim each time Dad got all dressed up to go out.

Now, she scrubbed at the draining board, energetically sending sprays of Sunlight soap up into the cold January air. "Anyroad, yer con get yer coot on and goo wi' Eva an' them," she said, giving me a push towards the door. "We'm right on rock bottom in that coal 'ole!"

"Ar, an we'n run out of ode shoes to burn an all, my wench!" Granny Coley called from the chair where she sat, wrapped up in an old army greatcoat. "It'll feel like corn in Egypt when yo gets back with some nutty slack!"

Only slightly placated, I put on my tweed coat and the pixie hat and scarf Nan had knitted that touched the ground. "C'mere." Eva deftly tied the ends around my back, strait jacket style. "Yow get that side with our Terry," she ordered as we began to push the unwieldly pram out towards the icy streets.

I had only been partly right about the way to the coal wharf being uphill. At the top of the "Mot" bridge there was a steep incline and the pram took off at speed, so that I more than once lost my footing and skidded under its careering wheels, banging my chin on the hard, wobbling handle.

"See that trolley?" panted 11-year old Terry, nudging me in the side. Turning my head, I saw a homemade box on wheels being pulled to the top of the hill by a lad I vaguely recognised from school. "Soon as our mother's dun wi' this pram, I'm mekkin' a trolley like that!" Terry bragged. "Yowr Dave c'n come on it, if 'e waents!"

I nodded, trying to feel pleased for my brother. I knew better than to ask if there would be room on the trolley for me. Some things, like fire cans and fishing in the cut, were exclusively for boys.

As we made our slow way home with the laden pram rocking from side to side, I passed the time day dreaming. Kathy Froggatt, who lived next door to the Millers, had come round to our house the night before talking about a special party in the street.

"We'm doin' it fer the Corrynation, see, cock," she told Mom, "Collectin' so's alll the little uns can 'ave a gud time on June 3rd!"

46

"So long as there's no 'ire purchise," Granny Coley still hadn't forgotten the shame of the returned gramophone. "We likes to pay we own road in this 'ouse!" she called out sharply.

As Mom sighed and quickly moved onto the doorstep, Mrs. Frogatt explained that a weekly collection would be made, sixpence for each child to provide for party food and drink, and a coronation mug to take home.

It all sounded so exciting. Not only were we getting a new Queen — Elizabeth the Second — but even the kids from the Lost City were to be included in the celebrations. All I hoped was that running out of coal didn't also mean we'd run out of money, because then Mom wouldn't be able to keep up the weekly payments!

CHAPTER
TWELVE

"We've just sid the QUEEN on a little box at me Nan's house!" I was so excited I didn't think twice about blurting out the news into my great aunt's crowded kitchen. Several heads, including Big Aunt Ginny's, swivelled round to stare at me.

"Awright for some!" Ginny sniffed, and then, curiousity fighting with the disinterest in her face. "Wor is this box then — a magic lantern thing?"

"No!" I frowned back, not quite knowing what a "magic lantern" was. "It's a television set! Yow c'n see pictures through it, an' Dave and me saw the Queen, plain as anythin'!"

It was, I thought privately, as I joined Rose on the rug, a million times better than the West Road Coronation party had turned out to be! Then, it had poured with rain, and all the children had been hastily snatched away from the tables and taken indoors by their parents.

"All YOW got was a dish o' trifle!" Mom couldn't get over it, and kept shaking her head. "All them tanners, to say nothin' of the new rigouts!"

I was still wearing my "rigout" — a red, white and blue cotton dress from the Friday night tally man's suitcase. I had thought it was beautiful and so original, until I saw Eva, Rose, and nearly every other small girl on the estate had an identical one!

Seeing the Queen on the television, though, was definitely something different! Forgetting that I could still be overhead by the rest of the family, I began to tell an open-mouthed Rose all about the wonders I'd seen "on the box."

"An me dad says we'll be getting a television of we own as soon as he c'n serve up enough money!" I finished, excitedly.

"Huh! From what I'VE 'eard, e's fun other things to spend that on, these past few months!" Big Aunt Ginny muttered, as if to herself. And though she steadfastly avoided my questioning gaze, I knew she very definitely intended me to hear!

Next day, I used the excuse of taking my library book back to go again to Nan's.

"It's my little wench! Come on in, darlin'!" I was glad to see that Grandad was at work and Nan and I had the house to ourselves. She brewed tea and gave me a slice of her homemade fruit cake.

"Yow look as if yow need five minutes love!" Arms around each other, we rocked together on the sofa under the baleful glare of the small television set which so transformed her tiny living room. "'is someut' the marrer, cock?"

I shook my head, suddenly quite unable to find the words to express the uncertainty I was beginning to feel deep inside. Nan looked more closely at me then nodded towards the magic box.

"See them potters 'ands!" We stared, fascinated at the lump of clay on the wooden board, being shaped and smoothed so gracefully before our very eyes on the screen "I know they purrum on fer the Interlude. But I could watch em all day!"

Leaning gratefully back against her apron, I drank in the peace being measured out by the gently ticking clock which had taught me to tell the time. In a minute, I knew Nan would be easily persauded to lead me upstairs to show me her "treasures", the lace edged pillowcases and the two plates with blue ribbon threaded through that had been a wedding present from her brother who was killed in the pit.

"Tell me about when yow was little, Nanna,." I said. Though I knew them all off by heart, those stories were better than anything I found in my books. I could see the little back to back house in Netherton, with the noisy family of ten brothers and three sisters and Nan, the youngest, who was always described as the "scraerpins up!"

In my mind's eye, I could imagine the cobbled yard, complete with privy and pig sty, and Nan's mother, Granny Smart, busily scrubbing the pig's back with a hard brush to make the cracklin' nicer.

As I later made my way over the steep Mot bridge, clutching the bag of toffees Nan had given me to take home and share with Dave, I felt I had been surrounded and fortified by love.

CHAPTER
THIRTEEN

"A box o' dried peas, please," I asked Jimmy Tarr distractedly. As I handed over the handful of precious pennies my mother had given me, I thought about the strained atmosphere at home where, for some reason, Mom wasn't speaking to Dad again.

I hadn't dared complain about going on the errand, or even look, hopeful of a penny, in Granny Coley's direction. She too had lapsed into silence, coming out of it only to sigh deeply and shake her head at her inmost thoughts.

Only the day before, while Mom had been busy black-leading the grate, I had sat and watched the mantlepiece clock for a whole five minutes, listening to its solemn ticking and amazing myself that Granny and I could both sit there and not speak for what seemed a very long time.

Taking the peas, I wandered out of the shop. The weather was warm. I knew lots of the bolder children would be swimming in the cut, enjoying the early evening sunshine. My Coronation frock felt heavy and itchy and the backs of my legs ached as I began to trail despondently back towards the streets of the Lost City.

On the corner of South Road, ahead of me, I saw a group of children, among them Janice Derby, whose proud boast was that she had "lamped" every kid, male or female, in our street.

Janice was short, squat and brawny, with a permanent scowl, and she always seemed to be surrounded by younger brothers, sisters and cousins. Up until then, I'd studiously avoided her, going numb with terror every time it crossed my mind that I might one day unwittingly become her next victim.

Now, to make myself feel better, I began to rhythmically shake the box of dried peas. I nearer I got to Janice and her posse, the harder I shook, my body soon responding to the beat, my feet skipping in order to keep up with it.

In a moment, I'd be safely past, round the corner and up the entry, giving the peas to my grim faced mother, who would be waiting, the water all ready for the overnight soak with the mysterious tablet of bicarbonate of soda.

"WHOOSH!" It was just as I drew level with Janice that it happened. The cardboard lid of the peas finally gave way and there was an enormous hard, greeen shower, falling all around me.

"SAFT bugger!" Janice's loud sneer rose over the screams of laughter of her mates. She came across the road, swaggering, pointing, as I stood gasping, trying desperately to snatch some of the fallen peas off my dress before they joined the rest in the gutter.

"Yow'll get a lampin' now!" she crowed, putting all my cascading horror at the thought of going home into spite-filled words. "Yer muther'll kill yer!"

It was my mother's face, twisted with fury, that swam before me as I turned on Janice, all my fear of her gone in the desparate heat of the moment.

"Oh, shurrup, YOW!" I shouted. "Oo the bloody 'ell d'yer think YOW am, anyway?"

I had one moment of glory as sheer astonishment made Janice gape at me almost like a frightened fish. Then her expression changed and she looked me slowly up and down — twelve months younger and a lot smaller. With no experience of fighting except the occasional spat with my younger brother.

"I'll get YOW, Carol Sheldon!" she threatened, one hard finger poking me in the chest. "YOW'll be sorry yow swore at me!"

I couldn't believe any of this was happening. But something told me not to cry, at least not until I was out of her sight. Clutching the empty pea box, I quickened my pace, needing to reach the safety of home yet reluctant to face what awaited me there.

"Hey, Carol!"

"Wheer's yer paes, Carol?"

"Wot yer throwed 'em away for?"

I tried to pretend Janice and her cronies weren't just a few yards behind me, catcalling and jeering. But when a stone, picked up from the gutter, caught me hard in the middle of the back, I couldn't ignore their presence any longer.

"See yer termorra, Carol." As I neared our gate, I saw a little group of women neighbours, gathered to talk in the pleasant evening sunlight. Janice's mock friendly parting had been, I knew, for their benefit, not mine. Head down, I passed through the women who suddenly seemed to have gone quiet.

I still had to face my mother with the evidence of the empty pea box!

Next day, I woke up early and crept downstairs before Dad went out to catch the coach. His goodlooking face broke into a grin when he saw me: "Bin in a bit o' bother, aye 'yer, our Carol?" he asked, knowingly.

I nodded resignedly and my heart thumped as I moved closer, thinking that in some miraculous, grown up way he knew about Janice and what she was threatening to do to me.

"I 'eard yow got sent ter bed early fer not doin' an errand right," he said, and as I nodded again, trying to hide my disappointment, he reached out a hand to touch my cheek.

"Dow worry, cock," he said, consolingly. "Yer Mom allus manages to find summat fer we tay — an' ter tell yer the truth, I cor stond dried paes meself!"

CHAPTER
FOURTEEN

"Dear Carrol Levis," I wrote painstakingly on the cream coloured writing paper I'd had for Christmas. "I should like to be one of your Discoveries . . ."

Though I didn't know the celebrity's address, and in any case had no money for postage, just writing the letter gave me comfort. When it was finished, I folded it carefully into an envelope and hid it in the shoe box under the bed when I kept my copy of *Little Women* and a red notebook Nan had given me.

In the notebook, I had written a story about a sad wireless set which didn't get played once its family got a television. That too, had soothed me, making me forget for a while that Janice Derby was still "after me".

But I couldn't ignore the way she had started following me, usually with two or three of her mates. Whenever I turned round in the school playground, she seemed to be there, a sneering, menacing shadow. But the worst times were when I came out of school and had to walk to the butchers or go up to the Co-op, where Mom had, unknown to Granny, opened a "strap" account.

Then the group walked almost on my heels, bumping into me on purpose by pushing one another into my back, while all the time Janice's grating voice led the tirade of abuse.

"Cross-eyed, knock-kneed, bow-legged — that's YOW, Carol Sheldon!"

"Scared now, aye yer? Yow bay mouthin' off now, bin yer?

"Yow wull be scared! Jus' wait till Janice gets 'old on yer!"

Shaking in my shoes, trying to outrun my persecutors, I almost wished Janice would beat me up there and then. It would be worth the pain just to get it over with. But my tormentor was obviously enjoying seeing me squirm!

There seemed to be no-one I could turn to, and I was sitting miserably on the entry wall when my youngest cousin Rose came along.

"Lo, Carol. Comin' out?"

It was the time for "Tin Can OLarky" and "Release," two street games I usually loved. But although West Road echoed with the shouts and running feet of my friends, I didn't dare join them. My heart felt as heavy, I thought, turning instinctively to library book land, as poor "Heidi's" had when she was taken down from the mountain and her beloved Grandfather, and had to sleep on a pillow that felt as if it were full of rocks!

"Nah!" I shook my head as Rose began to inexpertly throw two old tennis balls against the wall. Fairhaired and smaller than me, she suddenly seemed very familiar and comforting, and I found myself blurting out, "I cor goo in the street, Rosie! Janice Derby's after me!"

Even innocent Rose knew of Janice's reputation. Hastily putting down the balls, she hurried concernedly to my side. "Tell yer Mom — or yer Nan," she counselled, putting her small, warm hand on my arm. "That's wot Ar'd do . . ."

I looked at her, remembering the way Mom had been since Dad got back from Patsull and started his new job. Christmas seemed like a distant dream, and all I could think of was that she never seemed to stop working nowadays, and though she didn't complain about Granny and Aunt Maud, I knew taking care of them, and us, and the house gave her little time to think of anything else.

"'Er'd goo mad if 'er knowed I'd bin swearin' an' shoutin' in the street," I told Rose, seriously, my face going hot as I recalled the incident which had caused all the trouble. "An me Nan 'ud be ten times wuss! Ar'll just 'ave ter tek wot's comin' ter me, I s'pose!"

From Aunt Ginny's house, I suddenly heard the signature tune of "The Archers" wafting through the open window. That was the signal for my cousins to go indoors. A few moments later, I knew my own mother would be on the front doorstep, calling my brother and myself in from the tantalising, now scarey twilight.

"Yow could say yer WO fight!" Rose, obviously inspired, turned back to my desolate figure. "When 'er 'its yer, dow 'it 'er back! That sometimes werks wi' me an' our Joey!"

"Turn the other cheek," that was called, I ruminated, as I later followed my reluctant brother into the house, and in Aunt Maud's jocular words, "up the wooden hills to Bedfordshire." I remembered it from Scripture, when Mrs. Whitecraft sometimes got her favourites to act out Bible stories for the vicar to watch.

The message came, via one of Janice's henchwomen, that she would meet me the following Monday night. To say I was scared was the understatement of the century, and when I came out of school that afternoon, I scarcely noticed that the soft summer rain that brought a harvest of tiny green frogs.

My brother joined other, bigger boys, chasing and throwing them, but their cruelty had little effect on me. Miserably, I put my finger on the beginning of a chalk line that started on the corner of Spring Street and travelled the length of the power station's high wall. "Follow this line," was the smudgy instruction. At the end of the line, the words "You are saft!" mocked me.

I stared longingly at the smooth sides of the canal "stepping bridge" where children climbed high to slide down the bannister rail of blue brick that always reminded me of a giant elephant's trunk. I wished I could escape across the bridge, even though I knew it led only to another, larger council estate.

"Carol! Wait a bit!" Suddenly Eva and Rose were at my side. "Our Rosie says yo've bin offered out by Janice Derby!" she said, looking at me, wide eyed with unwitting new respect. "Er's on'y the Cock o' the street!"

"I know," I mumbled, aware that Dave and the boys were also taking notice. "It's tonight."

Later that evening, I stood by our gate waiting for Janice, my heart in my mouth. The word had got round that there was going to be a fight and I had even undergone a kind of training session in the air raid shelter, being told not to bite and scratch like a wench, but to punch 'er yed, cos her wouldn't be expectin' that.

Now, I looked around to see that the regulation square spaces in the concrete garden walls were full of children, friends and foes, all lined up as if they were in the best seats at the pictures.

As Janice, edged by her own supporters, towered over me and then struck — a hard blow to my stomach, I gritted my teeth. Resisting what the boys had told me, I thought fixedly of what Rose had said. If I didn't fight back, surely Janice would give up!

Sure enough after the second unreturned body blow, Janice took a step backwards and stared at me.

"Wot's up wi' yer? Think yow'm too good ter fight me?

Winded and dizzy, I looked up into her blurry, malicious face. The puzzlement she couldn't hide was, amazingly, to my advantage. So I stuck my nose in the air, and condescendingly shrugged my shoulders.

Maddened beyond endurance, Janice glanced back over her shoulder to her noisily disappointed mates. "Why dow yer run ter yer muther — ask 'er wot yer dad was doin' sittin' drinkin' in the pub wi' Eileen Dawson last wick!"

The words hit me harder than any blows could have done. I just stared, open mouthed, while Janice shouted for all to hear about my dad and his fancy woman that she'd heard her mother talking about, over tea.

"Lamp 'er YED, our Carol!" Dave called, as he came from down the entry. And his voice led a sudden roar from the bloodthirsty spectactors on the wall. "If yow dow, I wull!"

In the rage that engulfed me, making me fly at Janice Derby with furious fists and flying feet, I didn't need telling twice!

CHAPTER
FIFTEEN

"So now we've got the motor, me an' yer Mom thought we'd like ter tek the kids ter Yorkshire fer a few days — visit 'er sister Annie."

It was the longest speech I'd ever heard from Grandad and I looked up in surprise from Nan's sofa, where Dave and I sat watching "Whirlygig."

Dad had popped in to look at the second-hand Austin car that had appeared outside the house. I'd overheard him talking to Mom about US getting a car, too, but the dream had gone the way of the promised television set.

Squirming, I remembered what Aunt Ginny had said about his money, and how Janice's spiteful words about him being in the pub with common Eileen seemed to make sense of it.

"I'll goo an' see what Liza says," he promised now, as he went towards the verandah door. I longed to go after him, to ask if it were true what Janice's mother had told her, but I knew I didn't dare.

Instead, I tried to concentrate on the avuncular face of Humphrey Lestock on the flickering TV screen, while Nan hurried in from the kitchen, twitching with the excitement of her plans.

"We'll tek yer to see our Annie an' Alf, in Royston," she said, squeezing down between my brother and me. "Some o' my brothers am there — workin' down the pit — an' they've mostly got families o' their own be now!"

In spite of my secret anxiety about Dad, I felt my interest rise as I began to realise how much I hoped Mom would say we could go.

The trip was to take place during the last week of July, the first week of the industrial fortnight, when all the factories, including the Austin, closed down. Dave and I were both so excited we couldn't sleep, in spite of the hearth bath and intensified Friday night purges that we were given. Nan had made us both new flannelette pyjamas, and Aunt Maud supplied her old hop-picking suitcase for our few clothes.

"Ere, me babbies, 'ave some spendin' money!" Granny Coley called, busily unflapping her purse before we ran off to where the Austin stood outside our house, while Aunt Maud, beaming, presented us with two apples and two packets of Smiths crisps.

"Dow ate the blue 'uns! They'm salty!" she repeated the old joke over the visible blue twist of paper which contained the flavouring. We all laughed as if we hadn't heard it before, all except Mom, who suddenly looked anxious, as if realising for the first time that we were really going.

"See yer on Sad-dey," she said, as she awkwardly kissed us both on the cheek, and with a swift glance at Dad, who was hovering in the doorway. "Be-'arve yerselves, now!"

Head high, I walked down the entry, past the staring Millers, and Eva and Rose who had sneaked out to see us off while their mother watched, a tall shadow behind the net curtains. Did Aunt Ginny know Dad had been in the pub with Eileen Dawson? a little voice asked, tormenting me inside.

"Urry up, our Carol!" Nan's head poked out through the passenger door and I realised they were all waiting for me.

I had scarcely been out of Tipton before and was quite unprepared for the length of the journey to Yorkshire. The close confines of Grandad's pride and joy, his first car, made me feel sick, and I swallowed, trying to get rid of the overpowering smell of leather from the shining brown upholstery.

"Open the winder, quick!" Grandad hissed over his shoulder when I eventually confessed how ill I felt. He glanced at Nan, in her Sunday best in the passenger seat. "P'raps yo'd berra sit in the back with 'em, Soph! An' tek them rags an' perper bags wi' yer, just in case!"

"Ay we nearly theer, yet?" Dave, untroubled by travel sickness soon got bored and kicked at the seat in front.

"Course we ay!" Nan shot him an exasperated glance as she climbed in between us. "We'n still got the moors to get across!"

In between bouts of travel sickness, she tried to interest me in the panorama that soon came into view. "Look over theer, it's all gold," she pointed out, "and in another plerce, it's all black!"

Grandad explained that the difference in the landscape was due to weather changes, but as I drifted into an exhausted sleep against the bumpy, leathery back seat, all I could think was that he had left the Black Country and were now heading for a country that was shimmering and gold, like I'd read about in *Pilgrim's Progress*.

We stayed in Royston for four days with Nan's sister and brother-in-law in a tiny colliery house that seemed packed with people. "This is your cousin, Betty," Aunt Annie introduced me to a girl of about 12 and her brother, Max, who was nearer my own age. "You'll be sharing t'back bedroom."

Later Betty led me up the steep, narrow stairs to a room divided by a floral curtain. "T'lads'll be behind theer!" she said, then looking at me curiously. "D'yer live with yer Gramma, then?

'No." I sat down cautiously on the edge of the feather bed the two of us would share. It seemed strange to hear Nan called "Gramma," though I supposed that's what she was. "My Mom an' Dad couldn't come," I explained, smoothing the ruffled satin eiderdown. "They 'ave to look after my other Granny an' Auntie, an' they ay safe to be left."

"Oh." Betty gave a little shrug. "Let's go and get some spice," she said, mysteriously. "We can save it up for when they've all got to t'club."

"Haven't you ever heard of sugar and spice an' all things nice?" Betty's dad breathed beerily over me later that night when the grown ups returned noisily from their evening out.

We had passed the time sharing the sweets Betty and Max had taken us to the corner shop to buy. Much to my delight, we had also had singing and dancing, especially when Sheila and Jeffrey, two children from next door, had come in.

"Sheila and Jeffrey live on their own with their Mam!" Betty whispered confidentially, as we settled down on the snowy white bolster together. "Their dad ran off last year with his fancy woman!"

CHAPTER
SIXTEEN

My head was filled to bursting with all the new sights and sounds I had encountered in Yorkshire. But as the Austin took us home to Tipton, all I could think of was would Dad still be there — or would he have run off with Eileen Dawson?

"Yow'm quiet, our Carol," Nan noticed, from the passenger seat. "Not feelin' sick again, am yer?"

I shook my head. "Just thinkin' about gooin' um," I said, more gloomily than I intended.

"Er's SCARED!" my brother piped up knowingly as she fidgited with his woolly socks by my side. 'er 'ad a big fight wi' Janice Derby an' Janice sed er'd kill 'er, next time!"

Luckily, Nan was too busy pointing out the passing scenery again to really take in what he'd said. Giving him a surreptitious kick, I closed my eyes, reliving the moment when, sore but unbloodied, I'd emerged from my battle with Janice.

"Dow think yow've WON!" she spat, as the shouts of the audience told me that, amazingly, I'd done just that. "Cos I'll KILL yer what I see yer again!"

Just then, one of the quieter of our neighbours had walked past on her way home from weekly choir practice, and Janice had turned, sobbing piteously, in her direction:

"Oh, Mrs. Plant!" she wailed. "Carol Sheldon swore at me an' — an' now er's 'it me really 'ard!"

There, in the back seat of Grandad's car, I went hot with shame again, and my eyes filled with tears. As I relived Mrs Plant's shocked response.

"CAROL!" Horrified, she took in Janice's punched, and snotty face; the dishevelled state of our clothes and the spectators, still baying for blood on the council street walls. "And I thought you were such a REFINED little girl!" she said, before going, with a sorrowfully shaking head, on her way down the street.

It was then that I'd succumbed to tears, running indoors and straight up to bed to sob myself to sleep.

It was dark by the time we reached West Road that night. As soon as Grandad stopped the car I was out and running up the entry to the ever open back door.

"Where's Dad?" I panted, looking all round.

Mom stared at me. "Come in like yerself," she said. 'Ad a nice time, 'ave yer?" and as I again asked my fear-filled question. "Yer dad's doin' some overtime, but 'e'll be back any minute." she broke off and peered at me suspiciously. "Why?"

"I . . ." Relief flooded through me, making me realise how tired I was, and also how glad, in spite of everything, to be home. "I jus' want to tell 'im about Yorkshire," I lied, running back to the door where Nan and Grandad were struggling in with the suitcases and Dave was jumping up and down in his eagerness to see Mom. "We went over t'moors, an' 'ad spice, an' slep' in

Betty and Max's room, an' went to the Salvation Army on Sundey, an' the pictures on Sad-dey afternoon!"

"Calm down, yow'll werk the 'ousehold up!" Smiling in spite of herself, Mom put her work-reddened hand on my shoulder, and drew Dave closer into a hug.

As Nan and Grandad told her all the news from Royston, who had married, who'd had babbies, I was able to return in my imagination to the wonderful film we had seen with our new found cousins.

"Singin' in the rain! I'm Singin' in the rain!" As I sang the words in my head, I mentally joined Gene Kelly in his amazing, long distance tap dance to the lamp-post shower. It felt even better than being a Carrol Levis Discovery, and I couldn't wait for our next concert in the entry of 3 West Road.

But first, I had to face up to the retribution promised me by Janice Derby, and, more important, to find out if what she'd said about my father was true.

CHAPTER
SEVENTEEN

"On the wall, you will see a picture." Mrs. Whitecraft nodded her severe head towards the dunces' side of the class. The picture was directly above me — a picture of a boy with a toy sailing boat and behind him, a stretch of blue water. "You are to write a composition about the things you see in that picture."

I breathed out in deep satisfaction as the familiar, tingling excitement seeped into my bones. For the time it took to write the composition, I could escape the stuffy classroom where I now sat next to Wilfred Miller.

I could be with the boy and the sailboat. The boat might get lost, I thought, as I picked up my scratchy school pen, and dipped it into the inkwell. Or maybe the boy had just been given it as a present . . .

Wilfred, who was thin and sly looking with curling black hair, was shuffling at my side, fiddling around with the inkwell. And then, I heard Mrs. Whitecraft's voice again.

"Carol Sheldon! I trust you are not putting PAPER into that inkwell!"

"NO, Miss!" Even though I was innocent, hating the way the white enamel inkwells became clogged, I still went hot all over. I was aware that all the class was staring, and waves of disapproval were coming from the top end where Mary and Pamela were eager to start the project.

Mrs. Whitecraft picked up the inkwell, examined it, and my heart sank. There was no way I could "tell" on Wilfred.

"I think YOU'D better go and stand in the corridor!" the teacher said, plucking me triumphantly from my seat. "Go on! We can do without trouble makers in this class!"

"But . . ." As Wilfred Miller smirked, I left the class and went to stand outside, where I knew, sinkingly, that I would soon fall prey to Mr. Lodge. It wasn't fair, I ruminated. All I'd really wanted to do was write about the boy and his boat. As the door of the study opened and the stern headmaster came out and began to stride, glaringly towards me, I consoled myself with one thought.

Eventually the school day would end. I'd go home and sit by the fire with my red notebook and the indelible pencil that wrote blue when you licked it. Nothing on earth would be able to stop me writing the story then!

When I did get home that day, I was sent straight out again to buy some Fennings Fever Mixture for Granny Coley who had been "took bad."

"It'll bring yer temperature down, Gran!" Mom argued when Granny vehemently protested from her bed that she didn't want that "bitter tastin' muck." She paused as she straightened the eiderdown over the frail body. "If yow dow, yow'll 'ave to 'ave one of Big Ginny's kaolin poultices — or send fer the doctor!"

"No doctor comin' 'ere — an' as fer Ginny — er cun use 'er poultices on 'er gob!" the old woman muttered, then, turning to me: "Goo on then, Cock — fetch the Fennings, an' ave a penny outta the change fer some suck!"

"Spice." I said to myself, as I hurried through the back door. Our time in Yorkshire seemed an age and a world away and I tried to imagine what Betty and Max were doing now, while in the background the abandoned Sheila and Jeffrey still hovered. A reminder of the insecurity I carried around with me — and the promise I had made to get to the bottom of it.

When I got back with the medicine, Granny seemed much worse, thrashing around in her bed and mumbling about someone called "Old un!"

"That's wot 'er called 'er 'usband. 'e got burnt ter jeth in the pit." Mom told me anxiously. "Goo an' fetch yer aunt Ginny — er'll know wot ter do!"

Not needing to be told twice, I ran round to Big Aunt Ginny's where as usual all the children were in the back kitchen while their father ate his supper in splendid isolation in the front room.

"Mom says can yer goo in ter Gran — 'er's delirious," I said, surprising myself and them with a new word I'd recently picked up from a book.

Aunt Ginny was out of the back door in a flash, her outsize apron flapping round her, and her big hands bunched into fists. "I tode yer muther 'er wor well days agoo!" she called accusingly over her shoulder.

Taken aback, I stood for a moment, looking around me. Brenda was washing her long, dark hair in the sink,

71

the smell of "Drene" shampoo all around her. Eva sat embroidering, something she seemed to do a lot of since her mother told me, triumphantly, she had "become a woman" and wouldn't be coming out to play so much.

The boys, Joey and Terry were sorting through a pile of ancient *Dandy* and *Beano* comics on the hearth, and Rose? Rose was sitting under the table crying her eyes out!

"What's up, Rose?" Nobody moved as I got down on all fours and, moving across the newspaper that served as a weekday tablecloth, crawled under to join her. "Wot yer blartin' for?"

"I AY!" Rose protested, but her face was bleary and smeared with tears and snot, and she couldn't deny it for long. "Our mother's 'it me!" she finally burst out, as I handed her the hankie rag that, though unhemmed, my mother always made sure was clean. "'Er sed I'm disgruced the fam'ly!"

"Disgruced?" I squatted beside her, the legs of table, chairs, and children hemming us securely in from all sides.

"DISGRACED, yer saft bugger!" Dropping her embroidery with her mysterious new found "woman-hood", Eva fell onto her knees to join us.

"Yo' know the nit nuss come to yore school terday?" she whispered, "Well, our Rose got gid a NOTE!"

I stared, horrified, remembering the struggle Mom had, week after week, keeping my brother and myself free of head lice. Anything to prevent the frequently visiting "nit nurse" from giving us a note to take home to our parents. Those who WERE given notes were secretly shunned, looked down upon as Mr Lodge had encouraged us to look down on the boys with impertigo.

As far as I knew, nobody in our family had come home with a "note" and that included all Aunt Ginny's brood.

"Wot meks it wuss, though," Eva went on, as Rose, mortified, moaned aloud and covered her hot and sticky face with her hands. "Wot meks it wuss is our Rose cum all down the street — an' up the entry 'all excited — shoutin' 'Mom! Mom! The NURSE 'as sent yer a letter!' Our muther nearly killed her!"

CHAPTER
EIGHTEEN

The doctor said Granny Coley should be kept in bed and given "slops." I no longer overheard her and Aunt Maud grumbling in the night, though the snores were just as bad.

Aunt Maud had, in fact, begun to "wander off", tramping the streets with the rain making her white hair go frizzy and an umbrella forgotten in the bottom of her big black shopping bag. She began to talk about a daughter I didn't know she had, and one day the daughter, Elsie, came to visit.

"I thought I'd berra come an' see Gran," she whispered, meaningfully as Mom showed her through the gleaming front room and up the stairs. When she came down, she was shaking her smart, bubble cut perm and dabbing her eyes with a snowy handkerchief. "She dow look too good ter me, Liza," she said to Mom and, taking the cup of tea she was handed. "Er — yow an' my mother? Yer gerron well together, dow yer?"

There was a moment's silence as Mom finished wiping the draining board and putting the cosy over the teapot. Then Mom turned and met the other woman's rather shifty gaze. "Ar, we do, Elsie," she said clearly, suddenly looking taller and more in control than I had ever seen her. "But that dow mean I want 'er ter live wi' me forever. When anythin' 'appens ter Gran, I think it'll be yore place to tek yer muther, dow yow?"

Dad was at home, breaking wood in the coal hole and as Elsie flushed and nodded and said OF COURSE Aunt Maud should end her days with her, I saw him poke out his head and meet Mom's suddenly brave green eyes. Neither said a word but the look that passed between them spoke volumes.

That night, nobody seemed to bother to call us in from our play in the street and Eva, Rose and I took advantage of the extra time by inviting all the Miller children to watch us sing and dance.

A captive audience behind the wooden palings, they fidgeted or stared, and made rude noises while Eva and I did our famous interpretation of "I'll be with you in Appleblossom Time."

Rose still seemed downcast, and I somehow found myself sitting by her on the damp back step long after the Millers had escaped the concert and gone indoors.

"There's somewheer important I've got to goo, soon," I heard myself say, confidingly. "Yow c'n come wi' me, if yow like, Rosie — soo long as yow swear ter keep it a secret!"

My plan was to follow Dad next time he got all dressed up and went out in the evening. Then I'd know for sure if the whispers I'd heard about him and Eileen were true. I didn't know what, if any, action would come next, but just making a decision helped me feel better.

As Eva appeared, with strict instructions from Aunt Ginny that it was time to go in, I gave Rose a knowing look and made my own way indoors. Mom looked as if she'd been crying, and she told Dave and me that Granny was even worse.

"So be good kids 'an stay from under me feet, these next few days," she requested.

"Is Granny gonna die?" My brother asked as we got into our lumpy bed together.

"I dow know!" I snapped. "Er's very ode, ay 'e?"

Long after he'd gone to sleep I lay awake listening to the footsteps going back and forth into Granny's room. I tried to imagine dying — not being able to get your breath, or eat anything but the "slops" — bread and milk, weak tea and "Oxo" which were all the doctor said Granny should be given.

Then I thought of Aunt Maud sleeping with her sick mother, as she had done every night I could remember. What if she woke up in the morning and Granny was lying beside her, DEAD?

The only dead thing I'd ever seen was the day old chick Dave and I got off the rag and bone man when we were much younger. It seemed very sick and cold, and so we'd put it under the tea cosy on the warm grate. When Mom had lifted the cosy sometime later, she'd screamed, and the chicken had fallen out, dead.

Fitfully, I tossed and turned, and finally fell asleep to dream I was being chased by a big yellow chicken with Janice Derby's face.

CHAPTER
NINETEEN

When I got home from school next day there was a small crowd of neighbours and passers by standing by our gate.

"It's GRANNY!" Rose said, wonderingly, at my side. "Look — in the upstairs winder!"

We stood unnoticed and stared with the passers by as, through the open window, a scrawny arm waved a white handkerchief. Then Granny Coley's plaintive but still frantic voice blasted over our heads, "MURDER! Fetch somebody! They'm bloody clammin' me in 'ere! Tryin' ter kill me off in me own wum!"

"Slops!" I told the nearest figure, and my face went hot as I saw it was Mrs Plant, who had seen the aftermath of my battle with Janice. At the same time, restraining hands were seen taking Granny from the window and firmly closing it.

The crowd quickly dispersed, but indoors the shame had only just begun. Mom, her lips tight, had run round to Big Aunt Ginny's and was in the middle of asking: "Wot'll I do with 'er, Ginny? Yo' eard the doctor say nuthin' solid cos of 'er age an' state o' health . . ."

"Huh!" My great aunt cocked her head to where the sound of Granny's hungry lament was coming through her own open window,. "Ark at that! There ay much wrong wi' 'er state o' health now, is there?"

For the first time ever, I thought I saw a glimpse of something like compassion in her gaunt face as she looked at my mother's anxious one. "Ar'll tell yer wot ter do wi' 'er, Liza," she said, rolling up her sleeves to tackle the pile of potatoes waiting to be peeled by the stone sink. "Gi' 'er sum eggs an' baercon — a big plaertful! It'll either kill or cure 'er!"

By the next morning, Granny Coley seemed like her old self again, insisting on coming downstairs to sit by the fire while Mom went about her jobs.

"Ar, I bin poorly, Grainger," she told the old lady neighbour who looked in to see her with a bottle of stout. "One stage I day know whether I was on this earth or Fullers! But our Liza looked after me! Er's allus bin a golden wench ter me, an' allus wull be!"

Hunched over the stove, Mom seemed to be crying again. I went over and asked her worriedly what was wrong, but she just shook her head and turned away. "Goo an' spend yer pocket money. I'll be all right in a bit," she said.

On my way to Sid Tarr's, clutching the two brown pennies Granny had given me, I pondered on the strangeness of grown ups. Mom had cried when Granny had been going to die; now Granny was better she was still crying.

And things weren't getting any better with Dad. He and Mom had a terrible row the night before. I'd heard things falling over when he came home very late, obviously from the pub, and Mom had been "shushing" him until finally her voice was raised with his, and I'd lain in bed wondering where it was all going to end.

"Oi! Carol Sheldon! Ar've bin lookin 'fer YOW!" Everything seemed to freeze inside me at the now familiar taunting voice coming from behind me as I reached the corner. I stopped and turned and was face to face with Janice Derby. "Jus' thought yow'd like ter know I'm still after yer!" she called, as her cronies gathered round her like a flock. "Dow think yow scared me, jus' cos yow lost yer rag about yer dad's fancy 'ooman! I c'n still gi' yow wot for!"

"Oh ar?" Dimly, I saw that I too had been joined — by my brother, by Rose and Joey and Terry, whose slightly taller presence suddenly gave me new courage. "Come on then!" I challenged, scarcely aware that my little group was making encouraging noises. Only aware that Janice, after taking one step towards me, was miraculously backing off!

"Oh — I cor be bothered!" she finally said, shrugging exaggeratedly. "Yow ay wuth fightin' anyroadup!"

"Frightened o' gerrin another lampin', Janice?" Dave cupped his hands round his mouth and yelled after Janice's retreating back. "My sister'll bost yer YED in!"

Meanwhile, flushed with success and wanting only to sort out the other main problem in my life, I took Rose quickly to one side. "We'll goo ter that secret plearce tonight," I decided. "I'll meet yer in the entry at six. Aw right?"

Deciding how much to tell Rose was a problem, but in the end I didn't have to say much at all.

"Foller yer DAD?" she echoed, staring at me, eyes wider than ever. ''is it like 'ide 'n' seek?"

"A bit." Before I came into the entry, Dad had been busy at the sink, brylcreeming his dark hair and cocking his head to one side to get the parting right. He wore a clean white shirt and his one and only tie, a narrow striped one Nan had given him for Christmas.

Soon, Rose and I heard the sound of the back door shutting, followed by his faint but unmistakable whistle. "Quick — throw me the ball!" I hissed to Rose. Startled, she obeyed, and I caught the old tennis ball just as Dad reached us.

''Avin' fun, kids?" he said, preoccupied, stopping for a mere second to look at us. I threw the ball back to Rose. "Ar. Wheer yer gooin', Dad?"

Dad was nearly by the gate. He didn't look back at me as he said: "On'y fer a pint, Cock, — prob'ly at the Crown." Then, almost as an afterthought, he went on: "Yow be good fer yer muther. Goo in when 'er calls yer!"

"Right. Come on!" Pushing the ball into the pocket of my Coronation dress, I grabbed Rose's hand. By the time Dad had turned the corner of West Road and was heading towards Ocker Hill we were hot on his trail, careful to duck behind the solid garden walls if he showed the slightest sign of turning round.

"It IS like 'ide 'n' seek!" Rose giggled as we stood in Jimmy Tarr's entrance and watched Dad turn towards

Gospel Oak. He seemed to be hurrying now, obviously late for whoever he had to see.

One thing was certain, I realised, my heart falling like a stone. He definitely WASN'T going to the "Crown and Cushion" for a pint!

CHAPTER
TWENTY

"I cor goo along the CUT, Carol!" Rose plucked nervously at my arm as I tried to lead her in the direction Dad had gone when he finally left Gospel Oak road. "Our Mom's allus tode me to keep away from the cut!" she explained, agitatedly. "If ever 'er fun out . . ."

"Er WO!" Beginning to regret my decision to bring Rose, I looked fixedly at the purposeful figure now some way ahead of us on the canal towpath. Dad was heading towards a distant bridge and if he decided to climb back up to the road from there, I knew we'd lose him altogther.

"Look — we'll turn round an' goo 'um soon — honest!" I told the still wavering Rose. "But let's jus' see wheer 'e's gooin — okay?"

"Okay." Rose sighed and followed me through the brambles and down onto the quiet towpath. The canal gleamed, deep and mysterious waters lapping its brick sides in the quickly gathering twilight. There were bulrushes among which I knew the ducks had roosted for the night.

As Rose and I ran towards the looming bridge, I suddenly realised I wasn't at all sure where we were any more, and, more important, I had no idea what time it was! Under the bridge, a humped shape against the dank and dripping wall parted at the sound of our flapping footsteps. And became a man and a woman.

"Bloody kids — gerrout of 'ere!" The man's snarl was nothing like my dad's voice and I breathed a sigh of relief. As Rose and I blundered past, splashing in the puddles that had settled beneath the bridge's iron awning, the woman struck a match to light a cigarette, and I saw, to my utter amazement, that it was Mavis Derby — Janice's mother!

"I thought that'd be Eileen Dawson!" I said to the breathless Rose. Some instinct told me not to mention that I'd also feared the male figure was my Dad. Realising he must have disappeared into one of the pubs along the main road, I took her hand and we began to run home. The sky was still light, but I knew it was way past our time to be called indoors.

"It's a quarter to nine, cock!" a man coming out of the Crown and Cushion answered my apprehensive question sometime later. Rose started to cry then, and I stopped running long enough to shake her.

"Stop blartin'!" I ordered, now wishing with all my heart I had gone on my desparate mission alone. "They might not even've missed we, yert!"

But we both knew that was a very vain hope. Even before we turned the corner into West Road, we heard the voices, many and varied:

"Car-ul! Wheer am yer?

"Rose! Rose! Come in, Rose! Yer muther waents yer!"

The figures searching the gardens were illuminated in the opaquelly dying summer light. By the front gate, where she was scarcely ever seen, Big Aunt Ginny stood, arms folded across her ample bosom, silent with anticipation and fury.

"My kids KNOW they cum in after the Archers!" she muttered. "Our Rosie's fell under a bad influence ternight — 'er's very easy led, is our baby!"

I had time to register that the person she was talking to was my mother, who stood, rigid with shame and anger, at her side. Then, Rose was flinging herself at Big Aunt Ginny's apron front, sobbing:

"Oh, Mom — it wort me! It wuz Carol! 'er took me off, along the cut!"

"The CUT? Wot did I tell yer!" The crow was in the look as well as in the shocked and victorious voice of Big Ginny. I hung back, uncertain and terrified as Rose's sisters and brothers joined their mother and they bore her, still wailing, up the entry and into the safety of the house.

Then, it was just me and Mom, with her flashing green eyes and clenched mouth, and a moment later, hard blows, raining down on me. "Wot 'd yer goo OFF for, eh? Frightenin' the life out of everybody!"

I covered my face with my hands, my heart was in my mouth and I couldn't speak, even if I'd had the words. The force of her angry hands propelled me along the echoing entry and round the corner into our back kitchen.

"An' wot did yer 'tice ROSE off, for?" She shouted the name as she chased me, knocking over chairs, and falling down on the polished lino. Suddenly, illuminatingly, I knew she was doing this for Big Aunt Ginny's benefit — making sure that Rose's irate mother knew I was getting the punishment I deserved.

"You GOAT!" she screamed, oblivious to the startled noises coming from the old ladies' bedroom. "I'll learn yer ter do as yow'm tode!"

Thrusting me up the stairs, she pushed me through the bedroom door to where my brother, eyes like saucers, lay cowering in our bed. As the purposeful fists came, agonisingly, on my bare arms and legs, I suddenly found my voice. Knowing it was the only way to make her stop.

"I 'ad ter foller Dad! They say 'e's bin meeting Eileen Dawson!"

CHAPTER
TWENTY-ONE

"Eileen Dawson? Why should I be meetin' Eileen Dawson? I'm married ter YOW, ay I?

Dad's frenzied voice echoed through the house and I drew nearer to Dave for comfort. I ached all over from the beating my mother had given me and my eyes felt raw from crying.

As Mom, crying too, told Dad all she had extracted from me about the rumours I'd heard, I actually heard Dad laugh. But it was a sad and bitter sounding laugh.

"An' yo'd rather believe kids' tittle tattle than yer own 'usband! 'Onest ter God, Liza, I may've SPOKE to Eileen a couple o' times - 'er tried to get a bit pally when I was fust outta the 'ospital, an' I DID buy 'er 'arf a pint one Friday in the "Cup". But as fer anythin' else, iy's all bloody lies!"

"Well, I DOW BELIEVE YER!" Mom's reply carried, with her running feet, up the stairs, and I covered my face with the sheet. It was all like a nightmare, and the worst thing was knowing it was all my fault!

By the time Dave and I woke up that Sunday morning, the house was ominously silent. There was none of the usual smell of weekend cooked breakfast, and only Aunt Maud around, washing crocks from the night before.

"Mother's still asleep," she said, "soo I thought I'd get up and mek a start. I've done plenty o' washing up at the glassworks, ay I?"

I nodded and she peered at me. "Wot's up wi' yer ferce, cocker? It's all red and blotchy!"

"Er's bin cryin' cos our Mom lamped 'er last night," Dave replied, and then, looking around. "Wheer's Mom gone?"

Aunt Maud shrugged her boney shoulders. "Gone a' nuttin'!" she joked. "Gone to see Eileen, I 'eard 'er say!"

Fear clutched me. What if Mom had gone to hit Eileen the way she'd hit me? Somebody might call the police, and she'd be taken to prison! Numb with terror, I found a corner of the kitchen and just sat there, not even tempted out by the Weetabix and hot milk that Aunt Maud was making for our breakfast.

Nan would be expecting us for our usual Sunday visit, and I longed to be there, sitting on her old sofa, her arms wrapped around me for our five minutes' love. I closed my eyes, reliving the warm, encouraging things she'd told me about how Mom and Dad had got to know each other.

"Proper childhood sweethearts they was," she recounted, clucking at the affectionate remembrance. "In the serm class at school, an' everythin'. When they come to be married, yer mother day 'ave a penny to 'er name — bein' brought up by 'er old Gran an' all, so I set to an' med 'er frock, an' 'er was the loveliest bride that ever walked down the aisle of St Mark's church, an' the most pure!"

I wasn't quite sure what "pure" meant, though I'd heard it in reference to the Virgin Mary in our Catechism lessons at school, and it vaguely tied up in my mind with Lux toilet soap, which my mother always insisted on using on her face instead of "Sunlight."

A knock at the door startled me back to reality and a moment later, Terry and Joey came in to call for Dave. "I've got a set o' wheels in the shelter, fer the trolley!" the older boy said, as my brother hastily finished gulping down his breakfast and fastened the clasp of his striped elasticated "snake belt." He shot me a knowing look before saying to Aunt Maud. "Dow worry, I wo' tek 'im off nowhere . . ."

A moment later, Joey was poking his tousled head round the door. "Yer Nan's comin'!" he told me, his voice full of gleeful foreboding. But the words were music to my ears, as was the sound of Nan calling anxiously'. 'Lize? 'Arold? Why ay the kids come down this mornin'? Me an' Grandad's bin worried!"

As she entered the room, I flew at her much as Rose had flown at Big Aunt Ginny the night before, hiding my face in her warm side as fresh tears poured out of me.

"Why, what on earth's the matter, our Carol?"

Before I could reply, Aunt Maud, on her way upstairs with a brown paper bag full of pears, said, "'Er mother's lamped 'er. Don't know what for! I'll just goo an' see if Mom's awake"

Nan stared at me before taking me to the sofa by the unlit grate. "Now tell me all about it," she urged, "'As yer Mom really set about yer, or is yer face just red from cryin'?"

"I . . . " Torn between loyalty to Mom and the need to confess the terrible trouble I'd caused, I gulped and was unable to say anything except that I'd been punished for taking Rose off along the canal.

Just then, there came the sound of heavy footsteps coming down the stairs and to my amazement, Dad stood in the doorway with the suitcase he'd taken to hospital in his hand. He looked very pale and grim and he hadn't shaved. He didn't even glance in my direction as he said, "I'm glad yo'm 'ere, mother. I was just comin' down wum to see yer!"

"An' why the suitcase, our 'Arold?" Nan held me tighter as she stared across at him. In answer, Dad sighed and glanced around him in the trapped way I'd seen before.

"Me and Liza ay got a bit o' peace in this plerce," he said, "It's all werk an' sleep, an' now the Lost City bastards've spread it round that I'm seein' another woman! Turnin' me own kids against me!"

As his eyes finally met mine, I realised he wasn't angry with me at all, but at the people who had gossiped behind our backs. I longed to run to him, but his next words held me to Nan's side. "So I've decided, our Mom. I'm gerrin' out of 'ere right now! I'm comin' back ter live wi' yo' an' our Dad, wheer I belong!"

"AM yer, now?" Easing me gently to one side, Nan got up and walked over to where Dad stood, the suitcase at his feet. "Well, I've got news fer yo', our 'Arold," she said, her tone very measured and straight, so that each word met its target. "Yo' can allus come an' visit, an' what me an' yer dad can do fer yer, we always will. But as fer leavin' our Liza an'yer children, that's another matter entirely. Yo've med yer bed, my lad, an' now yo' must lie on it!"

CHAPTER
TWENTY-TWO

Mom had come in so quietly none of us heard her. But when I turned and saw her, I caught my breath because she looked so beautiful! Gone was the habitual scarf turban and smudgy apron. She wore her best frock, black crepe with cream inserts in the bodice, and her dark hair was rolled and pinned into curls around her head.

"Lize . . ." Dad took a step towards her, and I knew that, like me, he was fearful of what she was about to say or do. Wordlessly, Mom went across to the stove and poured herself a cup of tea from the perpetually stewing pot. She stood nursing it as she looked from Dad to Nan, to me. Instinctively, I drew closer to Nan, torn between love and the new fear that the thrashing of the night before had woken in me.

But Nan suddenly moved away. "Hark!" she said, going towards the stairs. "I think I 'ear Maud shoutin' we. I'll goo up an' see what 'er wants."

After Nan had gone, Mum seemed to find it easier to talk. She drained the cup and put it in the sink. Then she turned and faced Dad. "It's all right, 'Arold," she said, quietly. "I've bin to face yer fancy woman!"

Dad drew in his breath. 'Ow many times do I 'ave ter tell yer, 'er AY!" he began.

"I wanted to 'ear it from 'er!" Mom went on, evenly. "So I got up early, got meself dolled up, an' walked round to East Road."

"Wait a bit . . ." Dad shot a look in my direction. "Goo an' find yer Nanna, Carol," he instructed.

Responding to the warmth in his voice, I got to my feet, but Mom held up a hand which stopped me in my tracks. "No, I want 'er to 'ear this, 'Arold, as 'er's the one that 'ad to put up with all the talk!"

Mom took a step towards me, and I instinctively moved back. "Dow worry, cock," she whispered, and I saw the glint of tears in her eyes. "I won't hit yer again — EVER again, if I can 'elp it! I just want yer to know, it IS all lies, about yer Dad an' that Eileen Dawson."

She broke off and smiled crookedly in Dad's direction. "'Er as good as told me yo' was too old! 'Er might've tried to get off wi' yer once, an' let yer pay for 'alf a pint a mild, one night. But 'er's got other fish ter fry, an' yo' ay a patch on 'er new bloke, from Wensbry!"

It felt as if a great weight had been lifted off my chest. As the back door opened and Dave, Joey and Terry came in with the buckled wheels of an old pram for Dad to mend, Mom put the kettle on again.

She and Dad sat down with their tea at the table, and I knew without being told that now was the time for me to go about my own business. I'd go upstairs to my current library book, though it was a pity it was *Black Beauty*. I'd cried so much over the past twenty four hours I didn't really want to cry any more.

Upstairs, the house was cold, the stairs leading straight down to the front door, which was invariably left open. It was quiet, too, just the hum of Nan's voice, carrying on some sort of monologue from the old ladies' bedroom.

I was glad of the quiet after all the quarrels. It gave me an opportunity to think about all that had happened, starting with me beating Janice Derby and ending with Mom beating me. I knew that once I started to think, I'd start to write in the red notebook, and that whatever the story that came out, it would give me comfort, just as Nan's old fashioned Netherton stories always did.

"Nan!" My grandmother herself appeared so suddenly out of the dark bedroom in front of me I almost fell down the stairs. Her face looked different, somehow, set and strange, and she moved distractedly past me. "Not now, cock," she said, over her shoulder, as she hurried down the stairs. "I've got to see yer mother!"

I followed her instinctively back down and as the living room door opened, saw that Mom and Dad stood in each other's arms by the firegrate. Locked like the childhood sweethearts they used to be.

They only turned away from each other when Nan said, quietly, from the doorway: "I think yo'd best send fer Ginny, my wench. Yowr Gran's passed away."

CHAPTER
TWENTY-THREE

The day of the funeral, Mom sat in the back kitchen and cried and people kept coming and telling her she had nothing to reproach herself with. "Yo' did yer dooty by 'er, cocker, nobody can say any diff'runt!"

Sent out to play, Dave and I kept sneaking back to be fed ham sandwiches and slices of Nan's fruit cake. Nobody had suggested we went to the church. Instead, we had been left in the charge of Mrs. Grainger, who had "laid Granny out" and was also in charge of the spread.

"Yo'd never believe Coley was ninety one — 'er was in real good nick!" I overheard her telling another woman as they sliced and buttered bread in the crowded kitchen. "It was all I could do ter shut 'er eyes wi' the pennies!"

"Why'd yer do that, Mrs. Grainger?" I asked nosily, from by her elbow. She started, pulling a warning face at her companion, who murmured something about "little pitchers and big handles."

"Why, so's God c'n open their eyes in heaven, o' course," she said. "An' we use pennies cos they'm 'eavy!"

As I wandered away, I thought of all the pennies Granny Coley had pressed into our hands over the years. Heavy, cold coins that had soon grown hot and wet from our perspiration, staining our hands as we hurried up the hill to Sid Tarr's suck shop.

I remembered how, the night before, I'd lain in bed awake, long after my brother was asleep, listening to Aunt Maud talking to herself in the room she used to share with Granny.

"I'm gooin' to our Elsie's, yer know," she'd told me, yesterday, matter of factly, "So yo be a good little wench, after I've gone."

"I wil, Aunt Maud," I'd hugged her boney bulk a bit awkwardly, "But I'll miss yer!" I'd added truthfully.

"Ah well." The old lady pushed back my hair in an almost motherly gesture. "Yer Mom an' Dad deserve to be on their own now, an' besides, it ay the serm 'ere, not now Mother's gone . . ."

"Our mother says yo'll prob'ly ALL 'ave ter leave now!" As I wandered into the front room, shining with all Mom's extra efforts, I thought of something Eva had said when we gathered in the air raid shelter to talk about Granny Coley's death. "Yer Dad's name AY in the rent book, like told yer!"

Anxiety jabbed at me. It felt as if everything in the world was changing and I didn't know how to respond. If only I could go back to when Granny was still here, an aged but solid shape in the candle light. But to do that would be to return to the time when Mom and Dad weren't happy and I seemed to be carrying the burden of the rumours about him and Eileen Dawson all on my own.

The "spread" gradually disappeared into hungry mouths, and the beer the men had fetched from the off licence was poured into our few drinking glasses. Big Aunt Ginny and Mom worked for once side by side at both the kitchen table and the sink. They were standing at the sink when Granny Coley's long lost son, Gerald, came in and kissed Mom.

"Just as lovely as ever, I see, our young Liza!" he said, appreciatively, "No wonder our mother thought the world on yer!"

To his sister Ginny, he barely nodded and after he'd passed, she turned to Mom with a look that didn't try to hide her jealousy and spite.

"What yer gonna do now then, Lize?" she asked, craftily. "Move in an' lodge wi' 'Arold's mother?"

"Not bloody likely!" Shocked, I turned to see Nan, stately in her black funeral coat, bearing down on big Aunt Ginny.

Nan smelt as if she'd had a glass or two of the stout that was now being dished out in the front room. She pushed her way past Ginny and stood resolutely at Mom's side.

"Our Liza's gorra perfectly good wum 'ere — one 'er's worked damned 'ard for!" she said, as those nearest gave a small cheer. "We'm off to the Municipal buildings fust thing on Monday mornin' an' if they dow gi' our 'Arold the tenancy — I — I'll chain meself ter the railin's!"

It was twelve months after Granny Coley's death and Mom had finally found somebody to exchange council houses with us so that we could leave the Lost City.

"It's a woman 'oo's mother lives in South Road, an' 'er wants to be nearer 'er," she had explained, when she came back from one of her regular visits to the municipal buildings with a white card. "Oh, 'Arold, let's goo an' look at 'er 'ouse in Central Avenue — see if we can swap!" she pleaded. "The kids am gerrin' bigger now, an' I dow want 'em growin' up round 'ere!"

I frowned, thinking of the rag and bone men, the kids who threw stones in the summer and ice-packed snowballs in the winter, the dogs that hung, half starved, around the garden which were sometimes invaded by the rag and bone men's horses in the middle of the night.

"I always 'ad it 'ard," Mom admitted, as she sipped the Guinness Dad started bringing her as a tonic from his less frequent visits to the pub. "I want things to be better fer them!"

The new house was still in Tipton, at a place called Princes End. Dave and I hadn't seen it yet, but Mom and Nan were both excited and scandalised by the fact that it was "manky"!

"Never mind, we'll soon 'ave it clean!" Nan said, coming to see us with a pile of empty soap boxes from the Co-op. "Though 'ow Ginny'll like 'ER new neighbours, I shouldn't like ter say! They seem pretty manky to me!"

Big Aunt Ginny, tightlipped, asked no questions and heard no lies. But the day the removal van arrived to move us out, she arranged to have a big load of coal delivered, right across the front gateway.

"Ow'll I get to school?" I asked, as we climbed over the coal to help the removal van with our few things. "Is the new 'ouse a long way from St. Mark's?"

My Dad put his arm around me, and warmth and life flowed between us with the love that had no need of words. "We'll get yer theer," he promised, and then, as if struck by a sudden, illuminating thought, he threw back his head and laughed. "Hey, Carol, I ay tode yer Mom yet, but this plerce wheer we'm gooin' ter live now — they call it 'Abyssinia'!"

BREAD PUDDING DAYS

CHAPTER
ONE

"Ay 'is blood RED?" gasped the woman in the chip shop queue.

Transfixed with horror, I followed her gaze to where my brother had just punched a bigger boy squarely on the nose. Causing a great cry of rage, and big, bright crimson drops which had seemed to fly everywhere.

"So DOW say that to my sister again, right?" Dave shouted, as a small crowd, their chips forgotten, gathered round the spluttering, bleeding boy.

Before he could reply, I grabbed my brother's sleeve and stumbled, head down, back through the chip shop door. As we crossed Central Avenue and headed for the council house on the corner that was now our home, I wished he hadn't said anything.

As if reading my thoughts, Dave glanced up at me, the light from the oily street lamp illuminating the latest style crew-cut which was his pride and joy. "I'm glad I ay a wench, our Carol," he said, as he deftly unwrapped and popped a lump of black chewing gum into his mouth. "'Aving to grow them two funny lumps on the front o' yer!"

My face hot, I relived the way the boy in the chip queue had nudged his companion, a spotty faced youth

101

in a Davy Crockett hat, when Dave and I had gone in for the family supper.

"Look at them titties!" he'd hissed as, mortified, I'd wished the floor would swallow me. "'er day get them sittin' by the fire!"

Whatever that meant, he now had a bloody nose to take home — and we had no chips.

"Weer am they, then?" Mum turned, questioningly as we walked in, holding out her hand for the newspaper parcel. Dave and I looked at each other, united in our mingled shame and righteous indignation. Then, as I sighed and flung myself into the nearest of the brown leatherette armchairs, Dave explained:

"There was this kid 'oo med fun of our Carol's lumps — so I bosted 'is nose!"

Moaning aloud, I picked up my battered copy of *Wuthering Heights*, bought by my nan for my thirteenth birthday, and buried my head in it.

Dad, meanwhile, had just come in, parking the black saloon car that was his pride and joy outside the house. "What's up?" he asked, seeing Mom busy opening a tin of corned beef. "I thought we was 'avin' chips tonight."

"Change o' plan," she said, quickly. "Put some coal on the fire, somebody, while I warm the best butter an' get the table set!"

Over corned beef sandwiches washed down with hot, sweet tea, everything seemed better. I watched the fire flickering in the tiled grate and looked forward to later in the evening when Dad would switch on the television set with its funny, circular aerial.

"Yo'm quiet, our Carol." Dad looked at me a bit concernedly, and I swallowed, knowing that he musn't find out about the fight in the chip shop, and especially the reason behind it. It was all just too embarrassing. "Thinkin' about this new school they'm sendin' yer to?"

I nodded relievedly as I reached for another thick, white sandwich. It was nearly true. Since passing my thirteen plus exam, I had thought of little else but the County Commercial School, where I'd be going in September.

"We've gotta go to Wednesbury for the uniform soon, ay we, Mom?" The thought made me unaccountably nervous.

"That's right. Yours for the Commerial School!" Mom could hardly keep the pride out of her voice as she poured more tea.

"An' mine for Tipton Grammar!" Dave grinned and brushed his hand through his spiky haircut.

Mom met my eyes as we all remembered the unexpected triumph when Dave came home with news of his eleven plus success. "God 'elp 'em!" she said, fervently, as she stirred sugar into our tea.

Moving from the lost city council estate a couple of years before hadn't been without its traumas. Dad had told me that Central Avenue was part of an estate known as "Abyssinia" and it had certainly seemed a bleak and alien place to me.

"I know yow'll miss yer cousins, an' there's no air raid shelter to play in," Mom had said, as I stood, feeling desolate, by the uncurtained window of number

22, "But at least you an' Dave c'n 'ave yer own rooms now, an' it ay much further from yer nan's . . ."

Nan had been waiting the day we moved in, and between them the two women had unpacked the boxes and borrowed crates. Dad and Grandad had got from under their feet and were in the nearby "Tibbington" having a pint when suddenly there came a banging on the wall which separated us from our neighbour.

"What's THAT?" Nan asked, eyes saucer-like in her tired face.

Mom pushed her dark hair back under her scarf as she filled a jangling bucket at the sink. "It must be 'er next door," she said, sounding surprised. "Still, I expect we 'ave bin mekking a lot of row — with all the furniture movin'!"

None of us could quite believe it when the next night, the fierce rapping came at the adjoining wall again. Dad had gone off to his job on the night shift at the Austin motor works, and Mom, Dave and I were watching an episode of one of our favourite cowboy series on t.v.

"'Ark!" As Mom put her hand up and went to lower the sound on the nine-inch box, I was reminded of nights in our old council house on the lost city estate, when the electricity meter ran out, and we all sat cocooned in the necessary glow of the fire and candlelight with the benevolent shadows of Granny Coley and Aunt Maud moving around us.

The rapping sound came again, louder, more insistent. And definitely malevolent.

"P'raps the old lady ay very well . . ." I started to say. I'd caught a glimpse of our new neighbour the day before, a slight but straight-backed figure, thinly disguised behind pristine net curtains when our removal lorry had pulled up outside.

But Mom wasn't listening. Going into the front room, still packed with bags and boxes, she paced around, getting more restless and uneasy. "That woman across the road tode me today 'er next door's a tartar," she said, as if to herself, as I left Dave to the cowboys and went to join her. "They say 'er's drove one lot o' folks after another out of this 'ouse!"

"Oh no!" My heart sank as I looked into her tired but still sparky green eyes. "So that woman 'oo's moved into OUR 'ouse . . ." "As 'ad a 'appy release, as well as an exchange to be nearer 'er family!" Mom finished meaningfully, as she turned to a box of ornaments. 'Ere, Cock — tek this trinket set up to our bedroom, while I think what to do!"

I went as quietly as I could up the uncarpeted stairs. As another burst of intrusive banging came from next door, seeming to echo right through our house, I paused. Then, sighing, I went into my parents' room.

In the glow of the so far unshaded light bulb, everything looked peaceful and still, the green satin bedspread neatly laid, the big chalk Alsatian dog that had been Dad's best ever Christmas present lying in the window. As I placed the Woolworths glass trinket set on my mother's old fashioned dressing table, I hoped against hope that the "tartar" we seemed to have found ourselves attached to would just leave us alone.

105

"Just tek no notice, Liza — er'll soon get tired!" was Dad's advice, when he got up from his after shift sleep the next afternoon. "Yo've really worked 'ard to get we this place! So dow let 'er goo an' spoil it!"

"Er wo!" Mom promised. But all the excitement of our new home seemed to have gone from her, and she moved restlessly from room to room, dark head half cocked for the sound of banging.

At eight o' clock that night, just as the three of us were again beginning to watch another Western, it came, with such a ferocity that Mom seemed to caterpult to her feet.

Her face was pinched and white, her eyes like flashing emeralds as she paused to take off her scarf.

"Right!" she said, taking a comb from the mantelpiece and pulling it quickly through her wavy hair. "If THAT'S 'ow yow want to play it!"

"M-Mom?" Getting to my feet, I put out my hand, but she brushed it quickly aside.

"I shan't be long!" she said, firmly. Then, pulling herself up to her full height, she marched out of our house, through the gate, and finally, up the path to the house next door!

CHAPTER
TWO

"I never raised me voice," Mom related as she later sipped her cocoa by the dying fire. "I just told her this is my 'ouse, not 'ers, and if I can't 'ave me television on without somebody bangin' the wall, it's a pity!"

"So what did 'er say?" I asked, scarcely able to hope that this was going to be an end to the conflict. Dave, meanwhile, had taken a cushion and sat right in front of the television, something I recalled my nan saying was dangerous to the brain.

Mom took a look at my anxious face and gave me a quick hug. " 'Er said, all snooty like, 'then I suppose I'll have to learn to live with it!' Er's got a name, by the way! It's Mrs. Wills, an 'er's lived 'ere since the 'ouses was built. That's prob'ly why 'er thinks 'er owns 'em!"

"Yo ay jokin' about that, our Liza! That Mrs. Wills is knowed all over the estate for mekkin' folks' lives a misery!" It was the next day, and Mom was regaling Auntie May with the story of her taming of the tartar. One of the joys of moving to Central Avenue was that Auntie May, Mom's only sister, and her family of seven children, lived in nearby Ivy Road.

"Anyroadup," Auntie May said, as we all finished admiring her new baby, Susan, 'The reason I've popped round — 'part from seein' 'ow yo'm settlin' in — is to see if yo want to goo shares wi' me on some 'omework!"

"'Omework?" Dave pulled a face as he flicked through the worn comics he had just exchanged with Auntie May's son, John. "That dow sound very good!"

"Ar — that's wheer yo'm wrong, me lad!" Mom seemed brighter than ever, as she ruffled Dave's ducking crew-cut. "This kind of 'omework's what yo get paid for! Our May's been telling me all about it. It's putting hair clips on rods and cards for Neweys factory an even you kids c'n earn two bob a wick!"

The following Monday night, after Dad had gone off to the car factory as usual, the three of us went round to Auntie May's to collect our share of the work. "Yo'll need a pushcheer — there's a lot moor on it that yo think!" Auntie May's rather onimous voice was lost as she went to rummage in the indoor coalhouse.

My own eyes were drawn irresistibly past what seemed to be tons of strange looking metal rods to a figure that was slumped in the armchair. "Uncle Tom?" I whispered, aghast, as I took a step towards him. Auntie May's husband, back from his 12 hour shift at the foundry was like a living corpse, his face bloated, white, covered it seemed to me, in some sort of dust.

"It's all right, cock, it just teks 'im a while to come round once 'e comes off 'is shift!" Auntie May explained, as she shook a coal-covered pushchair open and handed it to my mother. "'E'll be bostin' once 'e's gor 'is boots off!"

108

"I thought 'e was JED!" Dave whispered to me, his eyes like dinner plates as we watched the two women loading the pushchair with an enormous pile of steel rods. Privately, I thought back to the story Mom had told me about Uncle Tom being brought up by a blind grandmother, after the death of his unmarried mother.

"The ode lady used to 'ave to go out an' beg in the streets to feed 'im!" she said, her eyes very sad as she probably recalled her own, not so different, impoverished childhood. "An' 'e never even 'ad a pair of shoes to go to school in!"

"Wake up, Carol!" Startled, I turned to see the pushchair now balanced precariously across Auntie May's doorway and Mom waiting for me to help push it. "The quicker we get these 'um, the quicker yo'll get yer two bob!"

It really was embarrassing, transporting that rocky load of Neweys clip rods round the corner to 22 Central Avenue, and I was heart sickeningly certain that every passer-by was staring and sniggering, especially the group of lads who stood on the corner of Ivy Road.

"We'll 'ave to stop up all night to to get these done!" I complained, as Dave also pulled a face. But Mom was cheerfully determined.

"Dow be ser saft! It'll keep we fingers busy while we watch we watch the telly! Yo'll see, we'll get through this little lot in no time!"

Four hours later, and way past my bedtime, I rubbed my tired eyes and stared at the tiny pile of steel rods which were all we'd managed to fill.

"Goo on then — gerroff to bed!" Mom finally conceded, as Dave and I leapt up as quickly as our cramped muscles would allow. Moving towards the mantlepiece, she squinted at the clock. "I'll just gi' it another 'alf 'hour!" As if coming round from a dream, she looked from the dead fire to the living room, completely taken over, as Auntie May's had been, by the ubiquitous homework.

"I'll 'ave to get this shifted 'afore your dad gets 'ome!"

"'E wo gerrin' otherwise!" My brother muttered, as he gave a sly kick at the pile of rods filling the nearest armchair. "I day know there was this many clips in all the WORLD!"

For the next few days, we struggled on, encouraged by the prospect of the extra pocket money Mom had promised us. With mine, I planned, I'd go to Blackhams bookshop in Great Bridge and browse for ages, before I finally chose. It was a luxurious thought that kept my sore fingers threading even when Mom herself started to flag.

"I dunno 'ow our May manages this, day after day, an' with all them kids to look after!" she complained.

"It's 'cos John and Graham an' all the others 'elp," Dave replied, wiping an oily hand on his forehead. Out of the side of his mouth, he told me, "They on'y get a shillin'a wick, but dow say anythin'!"

Had HE said anything about us getting two bob? I didn't get chance to ask, because just then, Dad came in from the fode.

110

"Lize?" he said to Mom, a note of desparation in his voice, as she looked at him as if through a mist. "Lize . . . If I give yer an extra ten bob a wick out me wages — wull yer promise ter get rid o' this bloody 'umwork?"

CHAPTER
THREE

Desbee's was an old fashioned ladies' outfitters shop right in the middle of Wednesbury. Its double fronted windows housed female dummies in sweaters and skirts, with bright scarves fashionably tied, cowboy style, around their necks.

Right round the inside of the shop stood swathes of material in all possible weights, colours and designs. The bell jangled as Mom pushed open the door, me trailing apprehensively behind up the worn stone steps.

"We've come for me daughter's uniform for the Commercial School," Mum told the rather forbidding looking asisistant. She pulled the piece of paper with the seemingly endless list of requirements on it. " 'is this the right plerce?"

"Yes, madam. School requisites upstairs."

As we followed her pointing hand and went up the curving staircase onto the upper floor, I was suddenly glad my brother Dave, who'd come along with us for the ride, didn't seem to have heard. He'd undoubtedly have said something loud and unneccessary about "requisites" not being on the list! Just like the time in the wet fish shop in fact, when he'd asked, in a puzzled, piping voice, whether "credit" had any bones in it. "'Cos that sign says 'credit will not be allowed'!"

"Stop daydreamin', Carol!" My mother's sharp nudge brought me back to the present. "The lady here's askin' you to tek yer frock off so's 'er can measure yer!"

"It's for the tunic, you see!" The thin woman who suddenly appeared in front of me said firmly as, all my apprehensions about this trip suddenly materialising, I undid my cardigan and took off my worn cotton dress.

Standing, shivering, near Desbee's upstairs sash window, surrounded by rows of school uniforms I suddenly felt more vulnerable than ever before in my entire life.

"Mmm." Flickering her tape measure expertly under my armpits, the assistant then darted away from me.

"Good job yo' put yer clean vest an' liberty bodice on this mornin'!" Mom hissed as I stood waiting, feeling like a goose pimpled beached whale. "I 'ope yo' washed under yer arms, like I tode yer?"

I nodded, conscious of the almost magical way her words seemed to have conjured up the smell of perspiration.

"Here we are!" The assistant was back, her arms loaded with navy blue garments. "We generally advise parents to invest in a generous size, madam," she told me. "I know she won't need a forty inch tunic for a couple of years, yet, but we do a very reasonable alterations service, and of course, tucks can be taken out as she — er — grows . . ."

My face burning, I submitted to having the almost floor length pinafore dress pulled in from the back, up at the sides, and in the lumpy middle.

"It's too big!" I tried to say, over and over, but neither of them seemed to be listening, until the assistant went off to find me a suitably large blazer to go on top of it.

Then, Mom rounded on me, her green eyes flashing sparks: "Now, yo can just stop moanin'!" she instructed, and nodding towards my bored looking brother. "This uniform's got to fit yer all through school! Dow forget there's Dave things to buy an' all. We ay med of money!"

At home, she got me to try on the tunic and blazer to show Dad.

"It'll mek 'er a suit o' jackets!" was Dad's comment, while my brother, true to form, muttered something about hiding lumps, then went back to his comic.

There was nothing my nan liked better than a challenge — especially if it involved needle and thread, or better still, sewing machine! My grandad had bought her the modern Singer hand machine the year we left the lost city, and she now spent most of her spare time creating wonders out of what she called "remdants" bought for a copper or two from Great Bridge market.

"I'll 'ave some darts in your gym slip before yo can say 'Jack Robinson'!" she told me, when Mom and I went to see her, laden with the heavy items we'd bought, as well as the maroon knitted sash and navy beret.

114

"Jack Robinson!" I said, feeling a bit better. "Look at the tie, Nan!" I held the maroon, navy and gold tie up under my chin. "We all 'ave to wear the same tie!"

Nan admired the tie, then turned to rummage in her old black shopping bag. "Now I told yer not to buy 'er any blouses, didn't I, Lize?" she reminded my mother, "I've bin down the market an' got this for the blouses — ay it nice?"

As she spread out the white material on the table, my heart sank. I thought of the school shirts I'd seen hanging up in Desbee's — all neatly pressed, all looking exactly the same. "There's enough 'ere to make yer two nice ones, "Nan said to me proudly. "An' with that bit o' shine in the material, they'll be somethin' different!"

It was no use trying to explain that being "different" was the very last thing I wanted when I made that important move to the Commercial School in September. As Nan went on to describe how she'd also got a bargain bundle of white tape and intended to write my name in Grandad's indelible pencil on it for all my clothes, I relievedly escaped to the backyard and the big wooden swing by the tarpaulin covered shed.

As I dragged my feet back along the ground then launched myself into the air, I could see inside the shed with its mysterious contents in tins and oily boxes, and on the counter, the iron "last" on which Grandad often mended our shoes, hammering in tiny nails and dull metal "dinkies".

I began to soar, the warm air wafting across my hot face and gradually my uncomfortable feelings about the changes in my life began to ease away like magic. I thought of Katy Carr, in the book that had soon become one of my favourites, and how she had fallen from a swing because her awkward Aunt Izzie hadn't told her the truth about why she shouldn't go on it.

Adults and children still had trouble being honest with each other, I ruminated. I couldn't tell my nan how badly I wanted ordinary shirts, and proper embroidered name labels from the Singer sewing machine shop, in Wednesbury. And my mom couldn't tell Dave or me that at least part of the reason she wanted us to go to these uniform wearing schools was because she hadn't been able to go herself.

"I passed for the grammar school," the swing carried me higher, right up into the cloudless blue sky as I recalled Mom telling us this story many times, as we'd got old enough to understand. "I was top of the class — top o' the school! But I couldn't go to the grammar because in them days, yo 'ad to buy all yer books as well as clothes. And Gran just couldn't afford any of it! Miss Jeffrey, the 'eadmistress come to see Gran — 'er was so upset — but there wore nothin' anybody could do!"

As I let the swing carry me higher, I knew now that Mom's unspoken need for us to do better in spite of shiny blouses and written name tapes was the spur that kept me reading any book I could lay my hands on. And that in turn kept me dreaming of one day writing some myself!

CHAPTER
FOUR

"Somebody to see our Carol." Dad looked suitably surprised as he came in from answering the front door, while Mom quickly put her empty Guinness bottle out of sight round the side of her chair.

I looked up from the hearth rug where my brother and I had been playing a very argumentative game of "Snap!" to see Barbara Phipps, a girl from school. Her mother, a tiny, obviously very energetic woman, came in behind her and began speaking at once.

"I found out wheer yo live from yer aunt Ginny — we'm from Ocker Hill, see — only our Bar's passed the scholarship to the C'mercial as well . . ."

"As 'er? That's good, ay it, Carol?" The relief in the air was almost tangible as Mrs. Phipps sat down and the adults started to compare notes about the intricacies of our changing from the secondary modern where we had both been since failing our eleven plus.

"What about the list, then?" Mrs. Phipps said, as Mom got up to put the kettle on. "An' the prices! I couldn't believe 'ow much I 'ad ter find, for 'er school mack!"

The school mack was one of the items we hadn't got yet, but in any case, I didn't want to think about it. As

Barbara, after a moment's hesitation, knelt down beside me on the rag rug, causing my brother to grab the "Snap!" cards and bolt for the back door, I looked at her.

Small and white skinned, with red hair, I remembered how, since we moved from St. Mark's juniors to Ocker Hill Secondary Modern, she had been teased about the colour of her hair until our teacher, Miss Harding, had taken the culprit boys to task.

"Barbara's hair's not ginger!" she'd said, her firm voice defying her delicate frame as she turned to the blackboard and wrote on it one word. "It's auburn. That's a lovely colour — and it reminds us all of autumn!"

"I'll be sorry to leave Upper Two A," I told Barbara, surprised at how easily the very private thought had come out. "Miss 'arding really likes we!"

"Ar." We settled back against the fender. It was almost like being back in the lost city where my cousins had never been very far away. "Do yer remember when 'er fust come — they all called 'er 'sos'?"

"S.O.S.!" I corrected, remembering how horrified I'd been when I'd seen our new teacher's almost skeletal figure in front of the class. "That means 'Save Our Souls,' but some of the lads said it meant 'Starvation On Stilts' an' all!"

During her time with us, Miss Harding had not only encouraged those of us chosen to take the thirteen plus exam. She had read *Tom Sawyer* to us on Friday afternoons — threatening to deprive us of it if there was any disruption during the week.

118

And she had suggested we make a class magazine, all written and run off on a Gestetner, and stapled together by U2A itself, and distributed throughout the whole school.

"Anyroadup," Mrs. Phipps, refreshed by her cup of tea, broke into our suddenly animated girlish chatter. "Me and Bar's dad was wondering — as these two'll be catchin' the same bus to Wednesbury every day — if they could travel together — keep an eye on one another, like. We'll get together again, the wick before they start, eh?"

By the time Barbara and her mom had left, taken home by Dad, whom Mom had rather grandly volunteered, it was time for bed.

I lay for a long time, listening to the sounds of the house gradually changing around me — the closing of doors and the switching off of lights. Warmth and security washed over me. As I fell asleep, I was glad that the next day was Sunday, with bacon and egg for breakfast, "Forces Favourites" on the wireless at dinner time. And Dad, coming back, red faced and cheery from the pub, to leave two taters, one each for Dave and me, all covered in salt and pepper, in the gravy on the side of his plate.

Our visit to the Phipps took place on a Saturday afternoon at the end of the school holidays. Mom, Dad, Dave and I all got into the specially cleaned car to drive the three miles back to Ocker Hill. As we passed over Cox's bridge, I could see rag and bone men's horses grazing on the thin, grimy grass, and in the distance, the shape of St. Mark's church, directly opposite the canal "stepping bridge" where my cousin Rose and I used to sit on Saturday afternoons and watch the weddings.

A pang of nostalgia bit into me, mingling strangely with the uncertainty I'd felt since the moment I learnt I'd been accepted by the Commercial School. Though only a few miles away by bus, Wood Green, Wednesbury, seemed a long way off and a whole world away.

Mr. and Mrs. Phipps were waiting, though Mr. Phipps, a tall, balding man, vanished into the garden shed not long after we arrived.

" 'E 'as to feed the ferrets," Mrs. Phipps said, matter of factly, as she ushered us through to the living room. "As it's a nice day, I thought we'd 'ave tea in the verandah!"

Mom's eyes widened with wonder and instinctive envy as, joined by Barbara, we were led through the back door of the neat, semi-detached house and into a glass-built structure full of trailing plants and wicker furniture.

"This is nice, ay it, 'Arold?" she said, as he rather awkwardly sat down. "Meks the one at yer mother's look like a pigeon pen!"

"A pigeon pen!" For some reason, this amused my pre-warned and previously well-behaved brother, who began chortling and flapping his arms. "Coo — coo — coo!"

As Barbara's mouth dropped open, I deliberately turned my back on him. "Tek no notice!" I said, as

Mom hissed at Dave to be quiet, and Dad threatened to box his ears. "Ee's saft!"

A few minutes later, Mr. Phipps came back, washed his hands at the verandah sink and joined us at the tea table.

"Come on, our Bar, yo' can 'elp me," Mrs. Phipps instructed, and Barbara disappeared, to come back seconds later with plates of salmon and shrimp paste sandwiches, and a chocolate cake.

"Thought I'd put on a bit of a spread — as we'm celebratin' the girls goin' to the C'mercial!" the little woman said, as she poured tea into china cups.

"An'our David gettin' into Tipton Grammar!" Mum put in as Dave, diverted from his antics by the food, bit hungrily into a sandwich.

"Ar, I was tellin' Stan 'ere, yowr lad's done well to pass 'is eleven plus!" Mrs. Phipps agreed. "We'm proud of the girls of course — but with wenches, it aye the serm, is it?"

"Ar," To my astonishment and fury, Mom nodded her dark head, as she looked from me to Barbara, now sitting side by side on the other side of the table. "Well, they do us'lly get married, an' then what use is their education to 'em . . ." she put in.

"Right, then . . ." To my surprise, it was Dad who, catching sight of my mutinous face, quickly changed the subject. "Let's gerrit sorted out about these buses ter Wood Green, then. What time did you say yo'll need to set out, Carol?"

"Twenty past eight." Over the past couple of weeks, I'd perused the timetable that had come in the post with my free bus pass. "If I catch the 265 from the bottom of Central Avenue it'll get me to the school just before nine . . ."

"So our Bar'd need to get on it at Ocker Hill at about — twenty to nine?" Mr. Phipps asked. "That'll be okay, wo it, cock?"

Barbara nodded. As we finished our tea, she seemed bored with the conversation and the arrangements. "Can I show Carol my record player, Mom?" she asked, and, without waiting for a reply, "Come on, it's in the front room."

The Phipps front room was cool even on a hot August day, and full of furniture, including a huge, ornate china cabinet. Standing on a table beside it was a square box emblazoned with the word "Dansette."

"I've got Lonnie Donnegan!" Barbara whispered, eyes shining with excitement beneath her auburn hair. "But they wo' let me play 'im in the 'ouse!"

"Then where . . . ?" Before I could ask the question, Dave was coming in to tell me almost triumphantly it was time to go home.

Sitting beside him on the slippery back seat of the car, I only half heard Mom wondering wistfully what it must be like to own your own house like the Phipps and to be able to afford to buy your kids expensive presents like record players.

I was suddenly realising. I'd never asked Barbara about the ferrets!

CHAPTER
FIVE

Dave and I walked down Central Avenue together, both feeling self conscious in our new school uniforms. At the bottom of the long street, just past Locarno junior school, we were to part company, he to walk to the nearby Alexandra Road Grammar School, me to catch the bus to Wood Green, Wednesbury.

As we passed the junction with Oval Road, our clumsy second-hand leather satchels (courtesy of Nan) banging against our sides, a hiss seemed to echo, gradually rising to a crescendo of mocking words:

"Grammar grubs!"

"Hey — grammar grubs — get out of our street!"

Dave wheeled, fists clenched, to face the taunters — boys of our own ages who were on their way to Park Lane Secondary Modern School.

"Think they'm posh, dow they?" called the only girl, whose socks were in grey pools around her ankles. "Bloody snobs!"

"Leave it!" I warned Dave, as I increased my pace and half dragged him along with me. "Yow cor get into a fight on the first mornin'!" My terror was that he would tear the new blazer with the Tipton Grammar badge that our mother had sewn so proudly — if a bit crookedly — onto his breast pocket the night before.

I'd never been called a "snob" before, though, and surprised by the label, looked back at the Park Lane girl. She immediately put both fingers to the corners of her mouth and, pulling it into a hideous grimace, made her eyes look as if they were crossed.

"Oh — bugger off!" I called, and had the satisfaction, just before Dave and I turned the corner, of seeing her mouth drop open and her stance go back to normal.

"Er'd betta not mess wi' yo, our Carol!" Dave said, with that hint of respect he'd never quite lost. "Yo lamped Janice Derby — cock o' the Lost City!"

Memories of past glory, especially such unlikely ones — brought me little comfort as I later waited for the bus which was to take me to my new school, and I felt very nervous, and very much alone as I watched my brother disappear round the corner that led to Alexandra Road.

Dropping the satchel onto the nearest wall, I stood in a queue that comprised office and shop workers, and only one other person in a navy blue school uniform. A small, white faced girl with long dark plaits who, like me, looked anxious and out of place.

"You goin' to the Commercial School?" she suddenly asked me as one of the men in the queue decided to walk and we found ourselves side by side.

I nodded. "Ar, there's a girl I know . . ." I still couldn't quite class Barbara Phipps as my friend,

"Gettin' on at Ocker Hill, but apart from 'er, they'll all be strangers to me."

The smaller girl smiled, "C'n I sit with you, then?" she asked, "I'm Janice Smith."

"P'raps we'll be in the same class, Janice," I said, hopefully, after introducing myself. As the bus finally arrived, we got on board, proudly showing our travel passes.

"I told Barbara I'd sit downstairs today," I said. Janice followed me and we sat right on the back seat, But tomorrow, we c'n all go upstairs, if yer like!"

Although only a few, clattering steps away, the upper deck, with its wide front seats and back row wreathed in tobacco smoke, always seemed very sophisticated. As Janice turned to me and nodded, I realised for the first time that, without Mom, or Nan, telling me what to do, I could sit wherever I liked!

At Ocker Hill, Barbara got on the bus, her school beret balanced precariously on the back of her head. "Our mother wanted to see me onto the bus," she puffed, as she took the vacant seat in front of Janice and me. "Good job I sid it comin!"

As we neared the top of her street, I caught the blurred figure of determined Mrs Phipps skidding to a halt in her chase after Barbara. She stood there, beaming and waving, while Barbara groaned and slunk down in the seat.

"Never mind," I said, unwrapping a packet of Beech Nut chewing gum and handing it round. "Er'll soon get used to it all. My nan on'y wanted me to bring me 'ockey stick an' tennis racket!"

Much as I loved my nan — in many ways the most influential person in my life — I was finding there were times when her slightly wacky but still dogmatic way of looking at things could be a problem.

"Bad enough carryin' these satchels an' when they'm full of books, it'll be even worse!" Janice put in, at my side. I quickly introduced the two girls, explaining that Janice lived in my street.

"That's nice," said Barbara disinterestedly, and as the bus bumped over the bridge at Leabrook, then took us past the Patent Shaft steelworks, "Anyroad, Carol, yo'll be pleased to 'ear, I got me dad to clear out the shed, an' mek it into me den. So, next time yo' come round, we c'n play me Lonnie Donnegan. I've got Paul Anka an' all, now!"

"Oh. Good." I didn't like to admit to not knowing who Paul Anka was. Instead, I thought again of the mysterious mention of Mr. Phipps's exotic pets, and just as the bus turned into High Bullen, I asked Barbara: "What 'appened to the ferrets, then? I thought they lived in the shed!"

In answer, Barbara frowned and blew a big bubble of Beech Nut. It splattered on her face, just as I could've told her it would, momentarily masking her freckles. "They've gone in a pen in the gardin, o' course!" she exclaimed. "Yo cor put ferrets in front o' Lonnie Donnegan!"

A few minutes later, the bus was making its way down Wood Green Road, past Brunswick Park on the one side, and on the other, huge, Edwardian houses which looked to me like mansions.

As we neared the bottom of the road, Janice suddenly said: "The Commercial School used to be just a big 'ouse — like these — well, two big 'ouses, acktwerly. They med up the 'Limes'. My dad was tellin' me 'e used to walk past when 'e was a little lad, cos my gran lived by St Paul's church!"

"Well, it's a school right enough now, "Barbara said, nodding and getting to her feet to ring the bell. "Look at all them kids!"

We got off the bus and stood for a moment as it sailed past on its way to Walsall. Following the direction of Barbara's eyes, I saw the big white building I had visited only once before was now crowded with figures in uniform — not on the raised bit which led to the impressive front door, and huge, double bay windows, but at the side, where there was an opening, now with iron gates, which looked as if it had been made for a horse and carriage to pass through.

"This must be where we 'ave to wait," Janice said, as we crossed the road and nervously joined the noisy throng of pupils on the cobbled yard. Inside the iron gates, I saw that there was a small doorway leading into the side of the building.

I licked my suddenly dry lips, remembering how, when Mom and I had come for my interview, we had been received at the front door. In his study, which opened onto green lawns and impressive copper beech trees, the headmaster, Mr. Donithorne, had turned straight to me and said, "Talk to me about dogs!"

I had been so taken aback that I'd stumblingly told him about every dog I'd ever known — from big Aunt

127

Ginny's undernourished mongrels to sad Greyfriars Bobby in a library book I was never going to read again because it made me cry so much!

As I spoke, I'd watched his expressive black eyebrows shooting up and down, then heard him begin to tell my mother that though I'd passed the written exam, it wasn't certain I'd get the place. "We have room for only 300 children, Mrs. Sheldon. Hence the interview!"

Were there only 300 children here? And what were they like? As the door in the side of the "Limes" suddenly opened and Janice, Barbara and I joined the very end of the surging queue, I wondered what on earth we had let ourselves in for.

CHAPTER
SIX

"Our rules are very simple," Mr. Donithorne said, as the newcomers all crowded into the school hall, a prefabricated building in the grounds of the house. "You go UP the narrow staircase near the back door, which used to be the servants' entrance, and you always come DOWN the big, sweeping staircase in the main hall. That's purely for safety reasons, and to keep the busy flow of school life all going in the one direction!"

The "one direction", as we were immediately to find out, was towards examinations called G.C.E "O" levels!

"You all failed your eleven plus!" our energetic new headmaster told us straight. "But you've been given another chance! All you've got to do is prove you're as good as the ones who DID go to grammar school — by taking your GCEs after three years of study instead of their five! That's why, every day, somebody here at the Limes will be nagging you about "O" levels! Now if you'd like to make your way into the lobby, your form teachers will collect you."

"Huh! Don't know if I'll like it, 'ere!" Barbara muttered out of the side of her mouth as we all filed out past Mr. Donithorne and into the pale September sunshine. "I 'ope we'm in the same class, Carol!"

We made our way around the side of the big white house and through the front door into the main lobby, where a woman and two men were waiting with lists in their hands. Turning my head, I saw that Janice had teamed up with a girl she obviously knew, and others too were recognising each other from previous school or neighbourhood links.

The noise grew to a crescendo until the woman, middle-aged with her hair in a bun and a pair of spectacles balanced on her nose, clapped her hands. "Please be quiet, everyone! And listen for your names! My name is Mrs. Alman, I'm the form teacher for 3Y, Mr. Ellis here takes 3X and Mr. Gregory 3Z."

I looked from Mr. Ellis — tall, stooping, with a friendly smile — to Mr. Gregory — a red haired man with a bristling moustache. Silence fell as the names were called, and soon I found myself, along with Janice and her friend Mary, following Mrs Alman into one of the big classrooms on the front of the house.

"Barbara's in 3X. 'er don't look very 'appy!" Janice whispered, as she pushed her long, dark plaits back over her shoulders. I turned to where Barbara, on the end of Mr. Ellis's group going towards the "servants" stairs was furiously signalling that she'd see me at breaktime. Then, I found a vacant desk, sat down, and put my satchel on to it.

"Right, 3Y!" Mrs. Alman closed the door and came and stood in front of us. The sunlight gleamed on her glasses, making her eyes seem suddenly very keen. All around, the school that had once been private mansions buzzed with activity and purpose. "First, I'll give you your timetables!"

"Times table?" My nan repeated, when, later that evening, I tried to comply with her demand to 'ear all about it!" "We did them — though I never could do nine times eight! Wor is it, our 'Arold?"

My dad, hurrying off to work, merely raised his eyebrows and grabbed the cardboard suitcase that held his nightwork "snap".

"Time table, Nan!" I grinned, taking the paper from my now laden satchel. "Look, we've got German on Mondays, double English Lit. on Tuesdays, an' something' called 'Stats' on Thursdays!"

"Yo'll 'ave double hernia by Friday, if yo'm luggin' all them books about!" Nan quipped. She broke off, and looked around. "'Ow's our David got on? Wheer is 'e, by the way?"

Mom turned from making a pot of tea. I thought she looked a bit pale and preoccupied, and wondered if she had been secretly worrying about us on this our first day at the new and auspicious schools.

"Like Carol, I think it's bin a lot fer 'im to tek in," she said, quietly, "but I sent 'im upstairs to change out of 'is uniform — which is what I want you to do as well, madam! Yer can 'ave a cup of tea, when yo come back . . ."

"An' a piece of my bread pudding!" Nan rejoined, as she took a greaseproof parcel from her bag and slapped it on the scrubbed top table. "I baked it today, specially!"

Running up the stairs, I found my brother standing on the landing in his old trousers, his twisted red and white striped "snake" belt obviously hastily fastened, and his once Sunday shirt buttoned up wrong, with one side of the collar sticking up round his neck.

On my approach, he jumped up and lowered himself over the bannisters so that he was hanging, monkey like, upside down.

"Hey, remember when we lived down the lost city — yo got scared listening to *Jane Eyre* on the wireless, an' me and cousin Joey 'id on the landin', an' when yow went to bed, jumped out, squaelin . . ."

"An I thought it was the "mad woman!" As I poked him playfully in his upside down ribs and passed on to my own room, I realised this was his way of letting me know. He wasn't too keen on the grammar school!

CHAPTER
SEVEN

"Three times around her little neck," Mr. Lynall, our English master read aloud from *Porphyria's Lover* by Robert Browning, and I felt a delicious shiver go up my back.

In the poem, the unfaithful Porphyria was strangled with her own hair, and the power and beauty of the language held me even more spellbound than the story of *Jane Eyre* had, on the radio.

"This is even better than *Tom Sawyer!*" I whispered to Janice, fidgeting a bit in the desk in front, her own long plaits hanging safely down her back.

The English lesson finished and we all gathered our books and prepared to move to another classroom, and for me, the misery of "Stats" which, even now I knew it was "Statistics", still made no sense!

As I took a seat at the back of the classroom, my mind still full of the powerful imagery of the poem, I thought how different school was from Central Avenue, and home. The elegance of the "Limes" had somehow been retained in spite of the prefabricated buildings in the grounds, and I never once passed down the sweeping staircase without imagining ladies in white dresses and long, Porphyria style hair, perhaps carrying the big, frothy hats they were going to wear in the garden. And apart.from the setting, the sheer variety of backgrounds of my fellow pupils made me wary as well as uncharacteristically tonguetied at times.

As Mr. Donithorne was fond of pointing out, the County Commercial drew children from as far away as Lichfield and Sedgley, all being prepared to travel in order to get a shot at those vital GCEs the system had thought it had deprived them of, when they failed their eleven plus.

"Join us on the back row! Are you asleep, girl?" I started back to the present realising that Mr. Barlow, the Stats teacher was glaring at me, and everyone else was turning and staring, some beginning to snigger.

"S — sorry," I hastily opened my books, and as he waited, eyebrows raised, "Sorry, Sir!"

It was a relief to meet up with Barbara at break and as we queued for our free bottles of milk, she complained about all the homework 3X had been set that week. "We've gorra write an essay about 'Myself in ten years time', an'we've got that maths from this mornin'! I'm beginnin' to wish I was back with Sos — ay yo?"

I hesitated as I pressed my thumb into the silver foil-topped bottle, silently weighing up the horrible stats and the ever present fear of somebody in games noticing my name tapes weren't right. Then I thought of Mr. Lynall again, and the way I could tell from the way he read it that he felt about that poem exactly as I did.

"No," I said, firmly, as I sat down on the nearest bench, overhung by the glowing beech tree. "Sos was all right — but this suits me better!"

Barbara shrugged as she took a packet of crisps from the smart blue duffel bag she'd started bringing in place of her school satchel. "Oh well!" she offered the bag to me. "Tek two," she said, consolingly, and then, as if suddenly remembering something: "Hey — why doncha come round again on Saturday? Ask yer dad to bring yer — an' we'll go in the shed wi' Lonnie!"

I nodded eagerly, and at home that evening, asked Mom if I could go. "We'll 'ave to ask yer dad," she replied, distractedly, as she shovelled "slack" onto the back of the fire to keep it in through the night, "but I dow see why not. We could all goo — for the ride!"

"Not me!" To my surprise, Dave piped up from the table where he was doing what seemed an enormous pile of grammar school homework. "I'm gerrin' me bike on Saturday!" he reminded us both. "Our John says I c'n 'ave it for two bob!"

Saturday dawned bright and clear, and after our usual shopping trip to Great Bridge, we had banana sandwiches for lunch and then Dad drove me to Barbara's at Ocker Hill.

"Yer mom's a bit disappointed. I think 'er wanted to see their 'ouse again," he remarked, as we watched Mom supervising Dave and his new bike, a real boneshaker from cousin John. "A bit o' keepin' up with the Joneses, our Carol!"

I stared at him from the passenger seat, where I felt really privileged to be sitting. "Dow be saft, dad," I said, innocently, "They ay nermed Jones — they'm called Phipps!"

He was still laughing and shaking his head when he watched me up the path to Barbara's house. "I'll be back about half past four," he called.

I didn't reply because I was too taken aback by the sight which met my eyes as the door opened. Barbara was wearing trousers — cut off just past the knee — in dark tartan. Her hair was all fluffed up and she had red lipstick, and a spotted cotton scarf tied round her neck.

"Like me 'air?" she asked, as she led me into the hall. "It's the Doris Day look!"

"Mm — yes," I replied. "Yow look a real bobby dazzler!" It was always my Nan's greatest compliment, but I couldn't tell if Barbara appreciated it or not. Taking my coat, she hung it up in the passage and I followed her through the living room, where her dad sat, reading the paper.

"Not too loud out theer, mind!" he warned, rustling pages.

"All right, Dad." Barbara said, sweetly, though she secretly raised her eyebrows in exasperation. "Mom's doin' we tea," she went on, as we moved on through what seemed the never ending rooms to the glass verandah. "We'm 'avin' peaches — an' evaporated milk!"

Mrs. Phipps looked up and smiled. "That's right, Bar," she said. "'Ello, Carol. It's nice that yo've come to play again!"

"PLAY!" Once we were out of earshot, Barbara tossed her Doris Day cut derisively. "Anybody'd think we was three instead o' thirteen! Dow worry about the ferrets — they cor gerrout!"

She indicated the row of wooden cages along one side of the garden. As we passed, I caught a glimpse, through the wire netting, of svelte creatures with large eyes and glossy cream coats.

"Me dad uses 'em to go rabbitin' wi' me Uncle Ted," Barbara explained, as I paused curiously by the cages. Then, with a flourish, she threw open the door of the green garden shed. "This is me den!" she announced. "Yo'm the first o' me mates to see it!"

Not knowing what to expect, I walked into the dry and clean interior and saw it was almost like a miniature house! There were a couple of garden chairs, a plastic rug on the floor, and, standing on its table against the far wall, beneath the gleaming window, the Dansette record player.

Breathing slowly in concentrated rapture, Barbara opened the lid, then carefully took a record from its sleeve. She placed it on the turntable, and lowered the arm, first turning the volume up full blast. A moment later, the whole structure seemed to shake as the vibrant, enthusiastic voice of Lonnie Donnegan split the calm, autumn air.

"Cumberland Gap — Cumberland Gap! Fifteen miles on the Cumberland Gap!"

The excitement of the beat was like nothing I'd ever felt before. Barbara and I beamed, and, just a bit shyly at first, began to clap and jump around. As we played the record again and again. And again.

"Know what?" she panted, as her grim faced mother finally hammered on the shed door and told us, through gritted teeth, it was time for the peaches and evaporated milk. "We could start we own skiffle group! I read it in last wick's "Marilyn" comic. All yow need's a tea chest — an 'ode washboard — an' a thimble!"

CHAPTER
EIGHT

"Cheese 'n' onion!" My mother repeated, as she busily fastened her coat and checked her hair in the mirror over the firegrate. "An' three spoonsful of tea and four sugars in a twist o' paper. All right?"

"All right," I replied from behind the book I'd borrowed from the school library. Though I'd never done in before, putting Dad's "snap" up for work sounded such a simple thing.

I peered at Mom before turning another page. "Where're yer goin', anyway? Why wo' yer be 'ere when 'e gets back from Nan's?"

Mom touched her nose with her finger in an almost playful gesture. "Never you mind!" she said, mysteriously. "It's a surprise! Now dow let the fire go out, our Carol — an' keep an eye on yer brother, on that bloody bike!"

The house went quiet as she closed the back door, and the sound of her purposeful footsteps in her trim high heels faded across the fode. Getting to my feet, I yawned and stretched, and decided I might as well get Dad's tea and sugar ready now.

Finding an old white paper sweet bag in the drawer of the tall, green kitchen cabinet, I opened the oriental style tea caddy and spooned not three, but five spoonsful of the loose dark tea into it. Then I went to the sugar bowl and carefully measured in six heaped spoons of sugar.

I'd twisted the bag shut, and was in the process of reviving my chewing gum when the door banged open and my brother charged in. "Catched yer, dippin' yer spearmint in the sugar bowl!" he crowed, "I'll tell our mother!" Then he broke off, and looked round. "Wheer is 'er, anyway?"

"Dunno." I took the chewing gum out and placatingly offered him half, but he shook his head. "I was just startin' Dad's snap. I give 'im extra sugar an' tea . . ."

Dave shrugged and dive bombed the sofa. "I come in really, to see if yer want a goo on me bike," he said, generously, "Well — to see if you want to learn to ride it!"

Turning from Dad's little suitcase, into which I had carefully put the now bulging sweetbag, I squirmed, part of me longing to just go back to the book I'd been reading, another, more secret and vulnerable part reminding me of my uselessness with things other kids seemed to take for granted.

Although thirteen years old, and as Mr Donithorne was forever reminding us, only three years away from leaving school, I had never even ridden a bicycle.

"Goo on!" Dave said now, getting to his feet. "Now's a good time — with Mom an' Dad both out — an' it's ever so easy!"

I hesitated, wishing I could make an excuse about homework, or having to change out of my school uniform. But he was right. There really was no time like the present!

"'Ang on," I said, remembering Mom's instructions, as he began to hurry eagerly outside. "I'll jus' put some coal on the fire!"

By the time I got out by the front gate, Dave had the bike all ready. Staring at it, I was appalled at the height — cousin John, who'd sold it to him, was several inches taller than me, let alone Dave. "It's got a crossbar!" I pointed out, nervously.

My brother regarded me with a moment's scorn before leaping onto the saddle. "Course it as!" he said. "I ay ridin a wench's bike — am I?"

Within seconds, he was demonstrating along the pavement, much to the disgust of several passers by on their way from work, first sitting, then to my open-mouthed admiration, standing with his feet on the pedals and his body high above the ricketty saddle. "Look — I c'n do a wheely!"

"Never mind all that!" I snapped, sheer terror making me irritable. "Just show me 'ow to start it — an' stop on!"

As patiently as he could, our kid encouraged me to climb onto the bike, which he steadied, and then to push my feet off the ground. "Just look straight in front, an' say one — two — three! an' I'll keep 'owt o' the saddle! Oops!"

The third time the bike fell on top of me, I suddenly remembered Dad's "snap". It was also, strangely, the moment I began to feel I might actually get the hang of staying on the machine, if only I persevered.

"Just a mo'," I told Dave quickly. "Gotta go in the 'ouse for summat!" Then I dusted off my scratched and battered hands, pulled up my oil spattered socks, and ran back indoors.

"Cheese 'n' onion," I repeated aloud Mom's very specific orders. Taking a piece of cheese from the pantry shelf, and an unpeeled onion from the plastic vegetable rack by the sink, I placed both in the suitcase with the package of tea and sugar and firmly closed the lid.

By the time Dad had come from Nan's and gone off again to the night shift, his "snap" on the back seat of the motor, I had progressed on Dave's bike to such a degree that I could stay upright for a few yards and he had begun, tentatively, to let go of the saddle.

As the time went on, the street got darker and we began to move automatically towards the nearest lamp post, on the corner of Laburnan Road.

"It's better down 'ere, there's more of a slope," Dave said, encouragingly, but I sensed he was getting a bit bored with the whole proceedings, and would be glad when Mom got home. He was also, I could tell, getting increasingly embarrased by my growing enthusiasm.

"There's no need ter say 'one two three' out loud!" he mumbled, as a couple of lads on the other side of the road began to nudge and titter. "Just tek a deep breath — an' goo!"

Gritting my teeth, I followed his instructions to the letter, and in the next few seconds found myself flying down Laburnum Road, luckily free of pedestrians.

"Pedal, our Carol — pedal!" My brother's frantic voice — filled equally with pride and worry — rang in my ears, then faded as the bike picked up speed and left him behind. The slope was more of a hill, and as for pedalling, I had no choice because the wheels were going round so fast!

Ahead of me in the red filled blur that had become my vision, I saw the pavement had turned into a road junction, with a chapel on one corner and the busy road leading across Summerhill Bridge on the other. All I knew was I had to stop — and I had no idea how!

"Brakes!" The word came like the answer to a prayer. In the second I hit the road, I pulled on the brakes. Next moment, I was flying right over the handlebars and landing with an almighty "thud" right outside the chapel — the bike, wheels whirring, landing yards away, upside down.

"I 'ope yo ay broke it!" I sat up, dazed and battered, to the realisation that the only part of me that seemed to be torn and bleeding was my right thumb! As my brother picked up the bike, and then, almost as an after-thought, turned to me, I got to my feet and, straightening my now filthy clothes, put the injured thumb instinctively into my mouth.

"Ay such a snob now, am yer — grammar grub?" The girl's voice was both familiar and unexpected and I turned in surprise as I began to follow Dave back up the road. She was sitting outside the chapel, her feet dangling beneath its surrounding railings, the girl who had cat called us on our first morning in our new school uniforms.

As I stopped and looked at her, she suddenly grinned. "I cor ride a bike, either!" she admitted, with a shrug.

"Ar well!" I grimaced at my still throbbing thumb and wrapped it in my none too clean hankie. "Ta ra, then!" I said, realising the importance of the moment.

"Ta ra," the girl replied, and almost as an afterthought, "I'm Joan."

It was with a satisfied, even light-hearted step that I caught up with my brother, and went into the house where we found our mother busy cooking bacon and beans for our tea.

"I fell off the bike," I said, in answer to her unspoken question as I ran cold water from the kitchen tap onto my thumb, dislodging dirt and gravel. As Dave danced about, suddenly full of the adventure of my amazing flight through the air over the handlebars, I looked at her lovely, smiling face. And remembered:

"Where 'ave yer bin, anyway, Mom? An' what's the surprise?"

Mom turned from the frying pan, the fork still in her hand. She looked from one to the other of us in dreamy excitement.

"I've bin to see our May's catalogue mon — 'e 'on'y comes round on a Wednesday night! 'An' it's all sorted 'an ordered. We'm 'avin' a verandah — just like yer friend Barbara's mother's. It'll mek all the difference to the 'ouse!"

Behind her back, Dave and I exchanged raised eyebrows, then eagerly followed her instructions to get to the table for our late tea.

144

It had been a busy evening for all of us, and it was almost time for bed when Mom, handing round the cocoa mugs, asked me, casually: "By the way, our Carol, 'ow many sandwiches did yer mek for yer Dad's "snap"?"

For once, the book was forgotten in my hand — the story I had secretly been constructing about a runaway bike and a girl called Joan disappeared like a soap bubble in my head.

"Sandwiches?" I repeated, horrified. And then, caught in the disbelieving glare of her astonished green eyes, I told her what I'd done.

CHAPTER
NINE

"I never could sew without a thimble, either," Nan reflected, as she rummaged in her needlework bag.

"It ay for sewin', Nan," I explained again, patiently. "It's for playin' the washboard with! I tode yer, me an' this other girl'm startin' a skiffle group!" Experimentally, I took the old, silver coloured thimble she'd unearthed, and, putting it on my finger, scoured it along the table. "Hark!"

"Stop it — yo'll scratch me formica!" Nan pulled a disapproving face and held up a reproving finger until I had put the thimble into my blazer pocket, where it couldn't do any more harm. "Never mind blasted skiffle groups!" she said, colourfully, as she finally sat down with our cups of tea and welcome chunks of still warm bread pudding. "Tell me 'ow yo'm gerrin' on at this new school!"

Placing my feet comfortably on the hidden ledge of the kitchen chair, I took a sip of hot tea, and, in between mouthfuls of the spicy pudding, described the "Limes", with its airy rooms and its wide variety of pupils.

Glancing at the "Singer" sewing machine up the corner, I thought guiltily of the daily discomfort I felt about my shiny shirts and handwritten name tapes. And how amazed and hurt Nan would be, if she only knew.

"Tell me about when you was at school," I said, quickly, my heart lifting as always at the prospect of a story. "Tell me about when yer run 'ome to scrub yer mother's floor!"

"Ar," Nan smiled, her hands around the china cup, her eyes laughing beneath the cap of white hair. "I was never a scholar, me. I used to let our mother tek me to the school gates, then, quick as a flash, I'd snatch off 'er shawl — an' run all the way 'um with it!"

"Once, the teacher sid me runnin' an' 'er shouted, 'Come back here, Sophia Smart!' But I just bobbed me tongue out like this . . ." Here, Nan obligingly demonstrated, "An' carried on runnin' an' by the time our mother got wum, theer I was, in the front room, scrubbin' away like a good 'un! Er couldn't complain about that, could 'er?"

Things were very different now, I reflected, as I later walked home, my heavy satchel banging against my side. Nan could never have imagined the homework both Dave and I had to do every night. It was probably for that reason that he disliked the grammar school so much — concentrating on his hobbies of bike riding and fishing with Auntie May's sons, our cousins John and Graham.

As for me, it was a good job I had the planned skiffle group to take my mind of things, I thought, crossing the road that led to Summerhill Bridge. Today, at school, Barbara had reported that she'd got an old tea chest off the uncle who went rabbiting with her dad.

"That's the double bass, then," she'd whispered, drawing me a picture as we sat in the hall for Assembly. "I'm gettin' a guitar for Christmas. So all we need now's the washboard, an' a couple o' thimbles!"

Fingering the single thimble in my pocket, I wondered if Nan might be persauded to part with another one. I knew it was no use asking for her washboard — she used it every week to scrub the collars of Grandad's shirts with thick yellow soap.

At home, there was great excitement, and at first, I thought it was because of me. "Whee've yer bin?" Mom demanded, looking up from the pile of potatoes she was peeling at the kitchen sink. "It's after five o' clock!"

I glanced at the mantlepiece clock which was always kept twenty minutes fast. It said a quarter to six. "I said I was goin' to Nan's tonight," I reminded her. "The bus goes past the bottom of 'er street!"

Sighing, I thought of how, since becoming conversant with the bus route, I would gaze most mornings down Walkers Street. Wishing I was on my way there, and not to Wednesbury at all.

"Anyroadup." Mom dried her hands on a tea towel and pointed to our quiet back garden. "It's come today," she said, triumphantly. "Me lovely big verandah! It's out theer in pieces — all it needs is yer Dad to put it up!"

Two days later, the girl called Joan stood by the railway bridge in Central Avenue and waited until I drew level

148

with her. "Wheer's yer bike today?" she asked, with a tilt of her small, narrow head.

I grinned and shrugged my shoulders. "Me brother's bike," I corrected, "An' 'e can keep it!" From nowhere came a well-worn phrase of my Nan's: "It's nourishment I want — not punishment!"

"Oh." Joan looked at me almost wonderingly for a moment. Then, she dissolved into giggles. "Yo should 'ave sid yerself, though — the way yo come down Laburnum Road, I thought yer arse must be on fire!"

Now, it was my turn to gulp, though the giggles weren't far behind. "I'm Carol," I said, as we paused for breath by a broken garden gate. "Is this where you live, Joan?"

Joan nodded, leading my gaze to a house with several cracked windows and net curtains which, even to my indiscriminating eye looked torn and filthy. The garden was a mass of waist-high weeds with pieces of discarded metal visible in several places. "Come in," she invited magnanimously. "Now I know yo' ay a snob, nobody'll mind!"

Curiously, I followed my new friend up a dark entry and into a kitchen thick with grease and grime. My feet stuck to the floor. There were cobwebs, dirty dishes, dirty clothes.

"Me mother ay back from work yet," Joan said, as she moved a pile of newspapers from a broken chair for me to sit on. "I've gorra do the claenin' up, but it dow tek long!"

As she proceeded to take a broom and sweep a pile of dirt expertly under the nearest rug, I looked towards the sink. There, coated in dust — obviously never, ever in use — was a small, wooden washboard!

CHAPTER
TEN

The verandah lay in the garden untouched by human hands for the next several weeks. Despite Mom's nagging, Dad couldn't seem to find the time, or the inclination, to begin the mammoth task of erecting it.

"I'll do it on Saturday," he promised one Monday as he dashed off to work. "I'll need to get the ode mon to 'elp me — an' prob'ly 'alf the kids off the estate!"

As Dave and I exchanged rueful glances, I wondered if Mom ever regretted going in for a structure that was definitely not "the size of a pigeon pen!" But it didn't seem so.

"We'll get the stove put in — an' the kitchen table 'an chairs," she planned, looking through the window over the sink onto the bare slabbed area — the "fode" where the verandah was to stand. "An' the sink, 'arold, that'll need movin'! There'll be room eventually for one o' them twin tub washers, when we c'n afford it!"

Finishing my German homework in the armchair by the fire, I pondered on the wonder of my dad's skills. Even with Grandad to give him a hand, I'd never realised he could do the work of a builder, gas fitter, and plumber!

Saturday came — and so did the rain — bucketing down in that unrelenting way that told us all it was "in for the day." "No good trying to put a verandah up in this, Cock," Dad said, trying unsuccessfully to keep the relief out of his voice as he stood by the open back door. "It'll just get ruined!"

Mom drew herself up to her full height, and I automatically flinched as her green eyes flashed fire. "Huh! It's gerrin' ruined out theer in the garden!" she pointed out, furiously. "Warped to 'ell, with all the changes in the weather! If I could put it up meself, I would!"

Remembering the time she and Nan had decorated our old house with vivid lemon spots that had to be washed off, I was silently glad that the verandah had to be Dad's concern.

Except that it wasn't. As more weeks went by it became almost like a battle of wills, with Mom complaining and threatening, and Dad placating and promising. While the grass began to grow around the wooden panels and through the holes meant for picture window glass.

"Dow mention the verandah!" became a password between my brother and myself, and we carefully made sure any visitors came in the front way and had no view of what continued to wait in the back garden.

It all came to a head the Monday I was off school with a bad cold. Mom had bought a sixpenny tape of aspirins from the shop up the road and was dosing me with them, washed down with orange juice, and sugar and butter, mixed together on a spoon.

152

As a knock came at the front door, she thrust the concoctions at me and wiped her hands on her apron. "That'll be the rent mon! Get that lot down yer while I let 'im in!"

The rent man was a tall, thin individual in a long, navy mack. He looked cold and miserable and merely sniffed when my mother tried to make conversation. "The card's all ready, theer on the table, an' I've put the money in it, as usual. — Not a very nice day, is it?"

Placing his black bag on the table, he opened the rent card, and after checking the amount was correct, put it safely away in the depths of the bag. Then he took a pen from his inside pocket and meticulously entered the amount Mom had paid on the card, and in his records.

"Yo'm still a wick in arrears, y'know, Missus," he said, matter of factly, and then, glancing at his watch. "I'll go out the back way. All right?"

Sheepish about the arrears, Mom nodded and led the way. From my invalid's position on the sofa, I heard the back door open and then the rent man's voice, raised in officious surprise: "And what'd yer call that, then?"

There was a moment's silence. Then Mom replied in the proud voice I'd come to recognise and dread these past few weeks. "That's me new verandah! Me 'usband's puttin' it up, as soon as 'e's got the time!"

"Can I have a look at it, please?" There was something about the formality of the rent man's tone that made me leave the warmth of the sofa and follow him and Mom through the ricketty gate and into the back garden.

There we all stood, with Mrs Wills's privet hedge neatly blocking one line of vision, while, to the other, stretched row after row of paling-edged gardens, some well-tended, others neglected, some sporting pigeon pens, and others scrawny, tied-up dogs. Shivering, I pulled my cardigan around me and watched as the rent man bent over, and with expert, unfriendly hands, examined the top of the piled up structure.

"Just as I thought!" he finally pronounced, while Mom fidgetted, frowning, all around him. "All wood!"

"That's right!" Mom relaxed, her eyes meeting mine. "That's what it sed in me sister's catalogue — produced from finest quality wood!"

The rent man glanced at her dismissively as he took a narrow beret from his mack pocket and levered it firmly onto his head. "Council regulations say no structures may be attached to council dwellings unless they are constructed with a base of solid brick!" he trotted out, as if reading from a manual. "I'm sorry, Missus. Your husband can't put that verandah up 'ere. It'll have to go!"

"GO?" As he picked up his bag again and made his way towards the gate, Mom caught at her breath and, giving me a wild, beseeching look, darted in front of him. Her hands bunched into fists and her eyes flashed with furious emerald, and I noticed he stepped automatically backwards. "but I'm payin' instalments on that — an' I got it all planned . . ."

With a final expression of contempt, the rent collector fastened the top button of his mack and patted his belt into place. "It's a pity you didn't consult the planning department at the municipal buildings then, Missus!" he said, sarcastically. "They you would've bin told what's what about planning permission!"

"Plannin' permission!" Mom repeated the two words in a horrified sigh as we watched our unwelcome visitor disappear down the path at the side of the house. "Yer nan said we'd prob'ly need plannin' permission, but I took no notice. Now what we gonna do?"

Neither of us looked at the ill fated flat verandah as we turned and went back indoors. I went back to the sofa, but even the unpleasant symptoms of my cold couldn't stop me concentrating wholely on Mom. Her face set and pale, she flitted about, straightening chairs and building up the fire. Finally, she put the kettle on the gas stove which now looked as if it wouldn't have to be moved, after all.

Making a mug of tea, she carried it carefully towards the front room, and the door that led to the stairs. "I'll goo an' wake yer dad up," she said. "It's moor or less time."

On Mondays, Dad always got up at lunchtime because he hadn't been on nights the night before. It gave him chance to get little jobs done, mainly on the car, before it was time to go off to Longbridge again.

Now, hearing raised voices from upstairs, I strained my ears, realising that of course Mom was telling Dad all about the rent man's judgement on her precious verandah. And he was responding, though I couldn't tell how.

A few moment's later, the figure of Dad came flying through the room, his braces only half over his shoulders, his thinning dark hair sticking up like a protest on top of his head. Close behind him, still clutching the mug of tea and wearing an anxious expression, came Mom!

"Calm down, 'Arold," she begged as Dad, his hands now fists, blundered to the back door and stared out into the garden. "What're yer goin' to do . . .?"

"DO?" Dad turned and stared at her before he suddenly took the mug like a man who would soon be needing substinence. "I'll show yer what I'm goin' to do! I'll teach i'm to throw 'is weight around 'ere! By next rent day, that bloody verandah will be UP!"

CHAPTER
ELEVEN

"This is Lope," Dave explained, matter of factly. "I've brought 'im for 'is tay!"

Tacken aback, Mom looked up at the tall, lanky lad in the grammar school uniform. He finished leaning his bike against the wall where Dave had left his, and came forward. " 'Ello, Lope. Egg 'n' chips all right?"

"Lo." He shuffled his feet and blushed crimson. "Yes — er thanks." As I looked up from my book, he acknowledged me with a barely perceptible nod.

"That's me sister," Dave supplied, "Okay if me an' Lope go in the front room, Mom?"

Mom's almost mechanical reply, about not making a mess, and changing out of his school uniform first was lost in the sound of their retreating footsteps. And soon, their noisy laughter.

"What're they doin' in there?" I asked crossly half an hour or so later, when the laughter had turned into insane sounding guffaws, burps and thumps.

Mom frowned, the paleness and preoccupation I'd noticed in recent weeks even more pronounced in her face. "When I took 'em some squash, they was laughin' about summat at school," she said, "I'm just glad 'e seems to be settlin' down theer at last. Go in an' tell 'em the tea's ready, will yer, cock?"

"Egg 'n' chips in the verandah!" I announced as I walked unannounced into the front room. "What yer laughin' at, anyway?"

The boy called Lope shot bolt upright in the best armchair. He looked as if butter wouldn't melt in his mouth. Meanwhile Dave was sprawled across the hearthrug, his face alight with delight and mischief.

"Lope's bin tellin' me about 'is stink bombs! E's got a whole box on em — and next wick, we'm gonna tek some into Monsooer's French class!"

At the new burst of schoolboy snorts and guffaws, I raised my eye-brows in older sister despair and went back to where Mom was busily setting plates of egg and chips on the table. True to her instructions, the old scrubbed top table we'd used at West Road was now in pride of place in the hastily erected verandah.

As Dave and his new friend joined me, I shut myself off from their fooling about by looking out into the dark garden beyond the big windows and bright curtains which Mom had somehow got hold of. I closed my eyes as I remembered the past week, when Dad had got up early every day and, face set with determination, grimly worked to put up the structure he had previously been content to let lie warping in the grass.

"I'll gi' 'im bloody planning permission, officious sod!" he'd panted on Saturday afternoon when he and a very taken aback Grandad had struggled to move the

158

sink — a process which involved a lot of bricks, pipes and obviously, unfortunately, water.

"Well, I'm sure we day need plannin' permission, no matter what yer mother says!" Grandad mused, wiping a line of dust across his lined forehead. "but things was different then — there was a war on!"

"Still bloody is!" Dad gritted his teeth, his brawny arms hugging the sink as if he were going to dance with it. "That rent mon'll find out about it an' all, when 'e comes again!"

"C'n we 'ave some more bread, Mom?" At my brother's voice, I started back to the present and realised for the first time that instead of eating with us, Mom was standing near the corner, where she said she wanted the gas cooker to stand.

"Where's your tea?" I asked, puzzled, as she obligingly went to the kitchen cabinet and picked up the loaf. I hoped she hadn't done without herself because of our unexpected guest, because it wouldn't be the first time she'd done that.

In answer, Mom brought the bread to the table. She shuddered in a way that though surprising was obviously authentic as she said, "I just couldn't face egg 'n' chips, some'ow!"

Over the next few days, the verandah was gradually completed. Plants were placed on top of the kitchen cabinet, the mirror with its comb box attached was screwed to the wall by the sink, the meat safe secured by the door. Finally, on the Saturday, Dad and Grandad performed the to me miraculous task of disconnecting the cooker and moving it into its new place.

"Ooh look, 'arold, how much room we've got now!" Mom was so excited — all the nigglingly worrying signals I'd been picking up completely turned off. She waved her hand around the once cluttered living room. "All we'll need in 'ere now is the three piece — the fold down table, an' the telly!"

She was right, I thought, for the first time glimpsing the vision. We might not have proper wicker furniture like Barbara's family, but with all the cooking, washing and eating going on out there, the verandah had added several feet to our living quarters.

So long, I thought, as I anxiously watched Dad frowning at the long black tubes that were on the back of the cooker, so long as we weren't all blown sky high when he turned on the gas again. And the rent collector didn't report us when he came round on Monday!

That particular Monday at school seemed to drag. Even my favourite English literature sessions didn't cheer me as I sat near the back of the class with the assorted members of 3Y.

"You all right, Carol?" Janice asked me as we trailed along, up the servants' stairs to History. "Yo'm quiet today!"

I nodded distractedly and was glad when the shrill bell effectively cut off any more conversation. What was happening at home, I wondered? Dad had promised to be up and waiting when the rent man called. To challenge him face to face with the fait accompli of the standing verandah.

What if there had been a fight — and the police had come, and Dad been arrested? My feverish imagination drove me relentlessly on so that I was scarcely aware of Mr. Gilson, our dashing History master, complete with academic gown, sweeping in to dramatically begin the lesson.

When school was over, the bus seemed to crawl and I never thought it would reach Central Avenue. But of course it did, and I jumped off, and, forgetting the bulkiness of the school satchel, ran headlong right up the long street to our house on the corner.

I heard it even before I came round the side of the house — the sound of laughter, and Mom's voice, full of pride and amusement: "Yo've never sin anythin' like it, our May! 'Arold just stood theer — wheer 'e is now, by the verandah door, an' 'e anded the rent man the card an' the money — an' the little squirt just took it as sweet as a nut! 'e never said a word!"

"So we can forget all about brick bases an' so called plannin' permission!" Dad put in. 'e was just throwin' 'is weight about!"

CHAPTER
TWELVE

"I'm goin' swimmin' on Saturday, to Wensb'ry baths," Joan said, as we sat together on the chapel wall. "It's on'y fourpence, if yer want to come!"

I made a swift calculation. Taking into account the twopence bus fare, I'd still have sixpence left of my precious shilling a week pocket money. — Surely that was too good to be true?

I frowned at Joan and offered her a piece of chewing gum. "Fourpence?" I queried. "I always thought it was eightpence in Wednesb'ry baths?"

Jean pushed her gum into her mouth then used her moistened fingers to tease her newly acquired Bill Haley kiss curl more firmly into place. "It is, if yo want a changing cublicle!" she pointed out, with an impatient "tut". "In the fourpennies, we all get undressed on the side. Saturday afternoon, it's wenches only."

"Oh." I swallowed, some of my enthusiam for the outing already beginning to fade. It was bad enough at school, having to get changed for hockey and netball, both of which I hated with a vengeance. Just the thought of stripping off all my clothes in front of other girls made me squirm with horror and embarrassment.

"Sometimes the chaps try ter look in," Joan put in, matter of factly, as she stretched the gum as far as it would go, out of her mouth, "but yo' just scream really loud — like this!" she demonstrated, causing several passers by the turn their heads. "An' they soon bugger off!"

The arrangement was that I should call for Joan at one o'clock, and on that Saturday lunch time, I dawdled down Central Avenue wearing my swimsuit under my clothes and feeling just a little less uncertain.

"Sit down!" Joan moved a pile of clothes, newspapers and an empty brown sauce bottle off the nearest sagging armchair, "I'll just get me things."

Grabbing a ruched yellow swimsuit from the sideboard drawer, she wrapped it deftly in a grey coloured towel that was draped across the fireguard. "Our mother's gone shapin'," she said, as she pulled on her coat and led the way through the grimy kitchen to the back door. "Me big brother's comin' 'ome today — we've bin claenin' up, specially!"

"Oh?" I said again. As we set off down the street, Joan chattering away at my side, I recalled how, during the weeks I'd been getting to know her, her big brother had featured largely in her conversation.

"I cor say 'oo 'e is, or wheer, 'cos it's a secret," she was saying now, even though I hadn't asked. Glancing across at her smaller, infinitely tougher figure, I wondered what she would say if she knew what my cousin Ann had told me — that it was common knowledge that Joan Hall's brother was in jail!

"Two fourpenny's, please." At the baths, Joan and I put our money down on the counter together. Seeing the change, I brightened up a bit. "We'll be able to get some cream pies from Teddy Grays after," I whispered.

Nodding gleefully, Joan led me through the side entrance to where the smaller pool was. "See, it ay too bad!" she said. "Let's find a space on the bench for we clothes!"

Turning my back on the figures in varying stages of undress, I quickly stripped to my swimsuit and was soon in the water, followed by an ecstatic Joan. We splashed around for a while until the pool got quieter and then my friend suddenly dive bombed her way to the side.

"Let's sneak in the eightpennies!" she suggested boldly. "The waerter's a lot deeper, an' bluer! I'll goo fust!"

"B — but . . ." Something reminded me I was twelve months older than Joan, and worse, this was Wednesbury, where my new school was. What if we got caught and Mr. Donithorne found out I had been trying to evade paying the right entrance fee? It was as bad as stealing!

"J-Joan . . ." I whispered, agonised, but she'd gone, darting like a wet rabbit past the pay desk, unoccupied now, and through the doors into the other pool. Shivering all over, I followed, conscious of the sniggers of several youths standing by the diving board, who obviously knew what we were up to.

"Come on! It's lovely in 'ere — an' it's wheer yo really wanted to come!" Joan pointed out her sharp reminder before she flung herself triumphantly into the warm water of the larger pool.

And it was bliss! Gradually, I forgot my conscience as I swam around, and it was only when it was time to come out, when our skin was white and wrinkly that I realised. Our clothes were still in the fourpennies!

"Dow worry!" Joan had become like a little heroine, staunch and fearless. She went and poked her head round the door. But was back in a flash. "The woman's on the desk!" she hissed. "We wo' both get past 'er! — I'll goo on me own!"

Dropping to her hands and knees, she scooted across the flagged floor. She seemed like an age. I stood in the changing room shivering, no towel, no clothes, certain that she must have been caught.

"Hey, Carol! 'Ere!" Just when I'd given up all hope, Joan's scrawny arms appeared, spilling over with clothes. With relief, I recognised my towel and skirt and jumper, which had all been piled up under my coat.

Shutting the changing room door, I began to search for my underwear, and within seconds, my heart had jumped into my mouth. "Oh no!" I exclaimed, calling out to the cubicle next door. "Joan — guess what yo've done!"

A few minutes later, we were back at the front desk, looking all clean and innocent, and anticipating the joy of Teddy Grays cream pies. But first:

"Excuse me?" I squeaked, trying to look like a girl who went to the County Commercial School. "As anybody lost these navy blue knickers?"

★　★　★

At home, things seemed really quiet and peaceful. Dave had gone out with his mate Lope, who turned out to be a mad train spotter. "They've gone to Crewe," Mom said, my my amazement, as Dad nodded from the other armchair. "'E's fillin' a little book with the numbers of the trains, like Roy does."

"Roy?" My adventures at the swimming baths were suddenly put into perspective.

"That's 'is real name, apparantly — Roy Loper!" Mom went on, and heaving herself to her feet, led me into the still pristine verandah. "Anyroad, you tek these pegs an' 'ang your swimmin' things on the line, while I tek your dinner off the pan!"

Surprised, I looked from the three wooden dolly pegs she'd handed me to the saucepan, bubbling on the stove. It had a covered plate on it.

"Cooked dinner — on a Saturday?" I queried.

Mom seemed to look awkward. Then Dad appeared at her side. "Yer Mom just fancied a bit o' stew, so I went down Great Bridge an' got some neck o' lamb," he explained. "There's some for yer brother theer, when 'e gets in!"

By the time I got back from hanging the wet swimsuit and towel on the line in the garden, my meal was all ready, the hot water still bubbling on the edges of the vegetable thick gravy.

Wordlessly, Mom handed me the butter dish, and I took a lump and mashed it into the delicious mixture. After the swimming and what had proved to be an hilarious bus journey home, I felt hollow inside with

166

an emptiness even three Teddy Grays cream pies had been unable to fill.

"Gerrit down yer while there's a good light!" Dad grinned. I knew he was quoting Nan, and recalled her telling me how her mother used to say the words and mean them, because she — great granny Smart from Netherton — had been brought up in the age of candlelight. And had never even be taught to read and write!

Dreamily, I spooned up the stew, only scarcely aware that my parents seemed to be acting strangely tonight, ignoring the t.v., hanging around in the verandah that gave us so much more family space. Glancing at each other with signals too strange and complicated for me to work out.

Finally, as I finished wiping my plate with a crust of bread, Mom blurted out, "We've got some news, Carol. We was goin' to tell you an' David together, but as 'e ay back yet — an' yo am the oldest . . ."

"What is it?" Fear brought me fully to the reality of Mom not looking at me as she picked up my plate and took it to the sink. Dad, meanwhile, had gone to the kitchen unit, and, standing on a chair, had become very interested in the nearest ornamental plant. I thought of how pale Mom had looked, lately, and how sometimes, she seemed miles away in thought, in a place where I couldn't reach her. "Is there sommut the matter with yer?" I blurted out, suddenly close to tears, as I got restlessly to my feet.

"No!" To my surprise, Mom caught my cold hands in hers and pulled me towards her in a typically awkward hug. "NO!" Her voice became a note of soft laughter against my hair, and all I could do was stare, my mouth dropping open as she explained.

"Why I've bin mekkin' changes — an bein' a bit funny lately, is because I'm expectin' another baby, Carol! You an' our Dave're 'avin' a little brother or sister!"

CHAPTER
THIRTEEN

"Yer can join our skiffle group, if yer like," I told Joan, as we walked back from the "Bruce" the following Saturday afternoon. The "Bruce" was the local fleapit picture house, only a street away from where we lived, and Joan had introduced both me and my brother to its dim and smoky interior, where much of the seating was on hard wooden benches.

Now, Joan frowned up at me, her kiss curl hanging lankly off her forehead, her small face smeared with orange ice lolly. "Whatyer mean, skiffle group?" she asked, suspiciously, "I ay 'eard on yer!"

I sighed and shook my head. "That's cos we ay prop'ly got goin', yet," I explained. "but there's me an' Barbara from school, an' we'm lookin' fer somebody 'oo c'n play the washboard. Yo've got one in your kitchen . . ."

"Ave we?" Joan's genuine astonishment made me almost ashamed of my sly manipulation. But then I thought about how pleased Barbara would be when I told her about our prospective new musician.

"Anyway, we can go to Barb's tomorrow, if yer like," I suggested. "Me mom says I can tell 'er about the new babby if I like!"

Joan looked at me sideways and sniggered as we turned the corner onto Tibbington Terrace. "Fancy yore mother 'avin' a babby!" she said, not for the first time. "Yer know what that means, dow yer?"

I pretended disinterest, but my face was already going hot. "It means they 'ad ter DO IT!" Joan informed me, and then, lowering her voice as we passed the policeman's house at the top of the street. "If it's a wench, they done it once — an' if it's a chap — TWICE!"

The fact that Joan seemed to know all about it didn't make it a subject I wanted to think about, much less discuss in the street. So I thankfully turned from the mysterious mechanics of the unborn baby's existence, to names. "If it's a girl, we'm gonna call 'er Victoria — an' if it's a boy, it'll be Nicholas!"

A tingle of delight went through me as I remembered how Mom, Dave and I had discussed baby's names as we sat by the fire.

"Our Carol's 'ad them names from books, I reckon," Mom had said, as Dave pulled a face and turned the page in his train spotting notebook. "But they both go nice with Sheldon, don't they?"

"I like Nick better than Nickle-arse!" Dave put in, receiving a quick clout from Mom for his trouble. He grinned, and brushed her light blow off his stubbly head. "Or Vicky — that sounds good!"

Since hearing Mom's news, we'd both taken more notice of little Susan, watching her crawl around the verandah when Aunt May came round to see how Mom was doing. It seemed impossible that soon it would be our own brother or sister, and I began to watch Mom anxiously wondering when signs of the baby's growth would begin to show.

At school, one of my new classmates, Norma, had told us a couple of weeks ago that her mom was having a baby. And so, I felt really excited when, going to Barbara's that Sunday, I announced at the door:

"Guess what? I'm 'avin' a little brother . . ."

"Or a sister, if they on'y done it once!" In the thrill of the moment, I'd momentarily forgotten about Joan. Now, as she followed me boldly into the Phipps' pristine back kitchen with her washboard wrapped in newspaper, and her baggy grey socks around her thin ankles, I saw as well as heard the dismay and disbelief in the air.

"Oo's that?" Barbara looked resplendent as ever in a new shirtwaister dress with a net underskirt that made it stick out so enviably I felt a weight in my chest. As she frowned down at Joan, two things happened at once. Joan wiped her nose on her sleeve and Barbara's mother poked her head around the living room door.

"Well, Carol," she said, in a tone quite bereft of cheer. "We didn't know you was bringin' a friend! P'raps yo'd better go straight to the shed today, our Bar . . ."

Barbara's round and usually pleasant face was tight and grim, her lips pursed as she led myself and Joan down to her precious den. As she threw open the door and stood back for us to go inside, Joan exclaimed: "Bloody 'ell! Dun yer live in 'ere, Bar . . .?"

"Course not — it's just for me music!" Barbara replied, supercilliously as she brushed past to go to one of the garden seats. "An' me friends . . ."

The word hung in the air as Barbara took a mirror from her voluminous skirt pocket and adjusted her auburn hair, styled as immaculately as ever. It was obvious I had overstepped bonds of friendship by bringing someone like Joan unnannounced.

"I — erm — asked Joan ter come," I gulped, for the first time really aware of the vast differences between the two sides of my own emerging world, " 'cos we need somebody to play the washboard in the group — an' 'er's got one . . ."

Taking the newspaper parcel off the strangely silent Joan, I unwrapped it to reveal the grey, dirt-encrusted washboard.

"Ergh . . ." Barbara curled her lip, and with an expressive gesture indicated she wanted the thing taken out of her sight. "Yer could've washed it, fust!" she said, shuddering. "I dow want a manky thing like that in my skiffle group!"

"Well, good!" Snatching up the offending washboard, Joan pushed it back into the creased piece of newspaper. "I dow know 'oo yo' think yo am — bloody snob!" she burst our, furiously, "but let me tell yer, I'm just as good as yow if not better! My brother . . ."

Raising herself up to her full four feet six inches, she stared from the open-mouthed Barbara to me who, speechless for once, was just wishing the wooden floor of the shed would open up and swallow me.

"My brother's on the wireless — 'Enry 'all the bandleader! An' as fer skiffle, well, I think it's rubbish! Cos 'oo I really like is Tommy Steele!"

"Er never even asked about the baby!" I told my brother, as we shared a bottle of raspberryade and a packet of our favourite fig bar biscuits before bedtime that night. "An' 'er was 'orrible to poor Joan!"

"Mmmm." Dave looked at me across the verandah table where we had previously been left to do our homework. "Hey — is Joan's brother really 'Enry 'all?" he asked, eyes wide. "I've 'eard 'im on the wireless, but I day know 'e come from Tipton!"

Exasperated, I poured out the last of the pop, measuring the glasses so that they were equal, and then taking a sip out of the nearest one to make double sure. "'e dow!" I replied. "It's just a story 'er's med up!" I broke off, thinking of Joan's obviously neglectful background and realised how lucky we were. "Anyroad, I think it shows 'er's got real imagination! Better than that spoilt brat Barbara Phipps!"

Next day, when Barbara got on the bus at Ocker Hill, she studiously avoided me, going to sit with a group of older girls on the ricketty back seat of the smoky upper deck.

Sitting with Janice Smith near the front, I heard them giggling, punctuated by Barbara's voice, low and authorative and finally collapsing into whispers that made them laugh even louder.

"You all right, Carol?" Janice glanced at me concernedly and I could tell she was wishing she was safely at school with Mary from her primary school, with whom she still spent a lot of her time. The atmosphere on the bus was distinctly unfriendly, and getting more so, the farther we got away from home.

"Dow worry, Janice, it's just Barbara bein' stupid!" I muttered as I steadied my satchel on the front window ledge. We were just passing Walkers Street, and if I craned my neck, I could nearly see Nan's house with the garage and the swing that I hadn't been on since I started at the "Limes."

A bolt of sheer longing shot through me so that all I wanted to do was get off the bus and go and see my grandparents, where I could be sure of a warm welcome and a lot of unquestioning, totally unconditional love.

But that wouldn't be possible until the end of the school day, and not even today because Mom wanted me to come straight home because we were babysitting Susan. I was thinking about Susan and trying to imagine Victoria or Nicholas — whose full names I still preferred to the shortened versions — when the bus pulled up in Wood Green.

"Come on, Barb!" the two girls who had been sitting with my erstwhile friend clattered down the bus on heels I knew they shouldn't be wearing. As Barbara walked between them, flinging me a triumphant look, the one at the back called out something that sounded like a foreign language!

"Urryha pua, atinsa hirtsa!" She looked straight at me before Barbara's chortle came back up the stairs followed by a shriek of mocking laughter from the girl in front.

"What did 'er say?" As Janice, red-faced, picked up her satchel, I grabbed mine and followed her down the noisy stairs and off the pausing bus.

Janice avoided my eyes, her face half hidden in the long strands of dark hair which, these days, she was wearing free of its babyish, restrictive plaits. "It's back-slang, Carol," she mumbled finally as we crossed the road to where Barbara was now in the centre of a staring, mocking group. "My brother showed me 'ow to do it, last year! An' I think 'er said — ' 'urry up, satin shirt'!"

CHAPTER
FOURTEEN

"Nobody gets it all right!" said my new friend Sally as we sat on the bench under the copper beech tree the next day. "My mother bought me boys' shirts — look, they fasten the wrong way!"

Sally jabbed her long, artistic fingers into the opening of her flat white shirt and raised her eyebrows meaningfully. "As for this Barbara, you're better off without her!"

Sally was very different to the fashion conscious Barabara. In fact, with her neat, Alice-band hairdo and her nice way of speaking, she was like one of the heroines in the tasteful, old fashioned school stories I'd started reading. Although we were both in 3Y, I had only observed her from afar until that morning, when, thanks to my newly pregnant mother, I had arrived at school nearly three quarters of an hour early!

"We've overslept!" Mom had announced, bursting into first my bedroom and then Dave's. "Get washed an' dressed quick, while I mek yer some toast!"

Going groggily downstairs a few minutes later, we were herded into the verandah, handed cups of milky tea to swig back, given a piece of toast, then pushed through the back door with our satchels and coats.

"'Urry up!" Mom called, as she waved from by the gate. "It's a quarter past nine by the clock!"

"That means it's really five to nine!" My brother tutted as he did the familiar twenty minute sum. Then he pushed his school cap into his pocket, leapt on his bike and rode off. "Yow're bus'll be gone! he yelled back, unhelpfully. Leaving me to realise that there wasn't a single child in Central Avenue except me. Not even Joan, who was very often late for her own lessons at Park Lane Secondary Modern.

It was only when I got off the bus, which thankfully had arrived at the stop at the same time I did that I realised something was definitely not right!

Now, turning again to Sally, sitting quietly beside me on the bench, I said, fervently, "Good job you was 'ere! I thought I'd gone saft when I come into school this mornin'!"

"Yes," My new friend smiled. "Fancy your mother thinking the clock said nine, when it was only eight!"

Something about her bright, intelligent face stopped me from telling her we always kept our clock twenty minutes fast, thus adding to the confusion. Instead, I repeated how pleased I'd been not to have to travel into school with the spiteful Barbara and her new cronies today.

"I might start catchin' the early bus every day," I said, a bit shyly, and then, looking at Sally curiously. "Why're you 'ere so early, anyway?"

Sally yawned and bent to pull up her spotless white socks. "I live in Sedgley," she explained. "So I have to

177

get two buses, and my parents have to set out early, so we all leave the house together."

"Oh," I replied, and tried not to show how instinctively impressed and taken aback I was, when Sally went on to tell me both her parents were teachers.

"They're not my real parents, though," she finished, matter of factly, as the first group of pupils began to come in through the side entrance. "I'm adopted."

"Adopted!" Throughout that day, I kept looking at Sally with her dramatically thick dark hair and brown eyes. How romantic it was, I thought — how sad and interesting, and absolutely different — to actually not belong to your family! Even Barbara's sidelong looks at break, and her snide, back slang comments about handwritten name tapes failed to reach me.

Not only was Sally Crowther adopted, she didn't care about wearing boys' shirts or getting to school three quarters of an hour earlier than everybody else!

When I got home that night, travelling downstairs on the bus with a quietly supportive Janice, I scarcely noticed my mother's contrite expression. "Me new mate, Sally, is goin' to ask if I can go to 'er 'ouse for tea on Saturday!" I burst out, as I flung my satchel on the nearest verandah chair. "'er lives in Sedgley!"

"Sedgley, eh? That's posh!" Nan had just arrived with an egg custard in her shopping bag. She gave me a hug.

"Fancy yer mother gettin' the time wrong this mornin'!" she said, "I can see I'll ave to give 'er some lessons, like I used to give you, our Carol!"

Dad glanced up from where he was shaving in front of the kitchen sink while, at the same time, Dave and his mate Lope were dismounting noisily from their bikes outside the back gate.

Momentarily, I wondered how Sally would fit in — if I asked her back here.

Mom switched on the television one night later that week and my eyes nearly popped out of my head with wonder and delight.

"The latest craze, sweeping the nation!" the well spoken but obviously excited announcer said. "That's right, boys and girls, it's the hula hoop — all the way from America, where rock and roll originates!"

On the screen, in front of my fascinated eyes, people of about my age and younger were making the plastic hoops spin and dance all around their hips! One girl had two, going in opposite directions, around her waist, while a tall boy made a hoop whirl wildly around his neck!

"I want one!" I told Joan that night, as we sat together on the Summerhill chapel wall. "It's like dancin' — only better!"

Joan paused a moment to adjust the spotted neckerchief she'd tied around her neck. "Everythin' costs too much," she said, momentarily sounding like one of our mothers. "This scarf was two an' eleven! It ay mine, neither, it's me big sister Pam's an' 'er'll lamp me into next wick, if 'er sees me with it!"

"Mmm. Wonder 'ow much them 'ula 'oops cost?" I mused. It couldn't, I thought privately as Joan and I got up and began to dawdle automatically home, be as expensive as trying to get a skiffle group together.

On the way home from school next day, I made a deliberate detour, getting off the bus at Wednesbury High Bullen and hurrying along to Woolworths, in the centre of the town.

I'd felt a bit guilty leaving Janice to make the rest of the journey to Central Avenue on her own. But it had also been immensely satisfying to see Barbara Phipps and her two mates staring at me open mouthed from the top deck. Wondering where I was going.

The hula hoops were on display in Woolworths windows — bright red, yellow, and blue, complete with pictures of young, ecstatic experts. "Get the latest. Only five shillings!" said the banner. Standing by the nearest counter were a whole pile of hoops, the top one a cheerful blue. My favourite colour.

"Yes, cock?" As overalled assistant came to my side, and I quickly turned away. The pockets of the overlarge school mack that had been the final piece of my expensive school uniform were empty, except for my bus pass.

Five bob! I thought disbelievingly, as I left Woolworths and headed back to the bus stop. At a shilling a week pocket money, it'd take me five whole weeks to save up for a hula hoop!

For the next few days, I tried to forget about it, but just as in my earlier life I'd dreamt of singing on the Carroll Levis radio show, and dancing in the red satin skirt Nan had made me, now I imagined making that bright blue plastic hoop spin so gracefully and expertly that everyone would be lost for words.

"Mom?" I asked, experimentally, on the Saturday dinner time. "C'n I 'ave a 'ula 'oop?"

"What?" She was busy ironing dry the shocking pink cardigan we'd decided I'd wear to go to Sally's and then found dirty on the bottom of the laundry pile. Staring up at her through the steam, I thought she looked really pale again and there didn't seem any sign of the presence of Victoria or Nicholas in her thin body.

"They'm five shillings from Woolworths," I went on hopefully, following her outside where she pegged the cardigan, almost distractedly on the washing line. I crossed my fingers as I told the lie. "Everybody's 'avin' 'em!"

"Ar — like everybody's 'avin' them Davy Crockett 'ats yer brother's gooin' mad for!" Mom sighed. Seizing the line prop, she sent the shocking pink cardigan skywards with what was definitely a final gesture. "Sorry, Carol, but we just cor afford these extra things — not now!"

"Not ever! "I thought, mutinously, as I stamped up to my room to find the red tartan kilt that definitely didn't go with the pink cardigan. Feeling really sorry for myself, I flung myself across the bed and squeezed out a few hot and miserable tears.

Maybe Nan would help me to buy the hula hoop, I thought, sitting up a few moments' later. But then I recalled that closed look on Mom's face, and realised it wouldn't be a good idea to ask. Mom would accuse me of going behind my back and besides, there was

Dave, and the fur-tailed Crockett hat to consider. Nan wouldn't be able to treat us both.

"Come in, my dear!" said Sally's mother, later that afternoon. "She's just finishing her piano lesson!" Looking over my shoulder, she extended the invitation to Dad, who'd been persauded to take me to Sedgley in the car. "Pleased to meet you, Mr. Sheldon!"

"And you, Mrs, er . . ." Dad mumbled shyly. Taking a step backwards onto the gravel drive, he said. "I'll come back for 'er about six, then. Then he looked at me, and, to my dismay, said, "Be'erve yerself!"

Mrs. Crowther led me through a hallway illuminated by the stained glass over the door panel. "Let me take your coat, Carol," she offered, and as a door opened. "Ah, here's Sally now! How did you do today, darling?"

Sally grinned a bit self consciously and gave a little, modest shrug as a tall man with a beard patted her mother's arm and reached for his homberg from the hat stand. "She was excellent as ever, Mrs. Crowther," he said, "You have a very talented young lady here — not only the piano, but the piano accordian, eh?"

After he had left, Sally's mom went into the kitchen to get us a drink and I followed Sally into the room where she had been playing. It was a room like none I had ever seen before, with a high ceiling, plaster coving and a magnificent marble fireplace which held a screen painted with flowers that looked real. The windows were wide, with drapes made of some sort of pale material, and the furniture looked as spotless as it was expensive.

182

In an alcove, stood the piano, its lid open, and I thought immediately of the only pianist I'd ever really heard of — Beth March in what used to be my very favourite book, *Little Women*.

"Can you really play that an' somethin' else?" I asked Sally, admiringly.

She nodded. "Only 'cos I've had lessons for about a million years!" she said, matter of factly. Picking up the heavy looking accordian off the the floor, she slid its straps over her thin shoulders. "S'pose I'll have to let you hear it, or I'll never have any peace!"

The time passed quickly and soon we were being collected by Sally's mother to go into the dining room for tea. Her dad was home by then, a tall, prematurely grey haired man who reminded me of our doctor. As I sat with him at the tastefully laid table, I felt tongue tied and as clumsy as a baby elephant. In spite of all Mom's efforts, the shocking pink cardigan still felt damp around the neck, and the colour was screaming at the red tartan kilt.

"So, what do you like to do in your spare time, then, Carol?" Mr. Crowther smiled interestedly across at me, as he handed me the bread and butter.

"I . . ." There was a pregnant pause while I swallowed the lump of tinned pear I had been trying to chew quietly. "Well, I like readin'," I replied, truthfully. "I — er — sometimes write stories an' — an' I'm an expert with the 'ula 'oop!"

CHAPTER
FIFTEEN

Sally came to my house the following Saturday, arriving by bus just as Mom had finished tidying up. "No, we haven't got a car," she said, as she sat down in the armchair nearest the fire. "My dad always says there are other priorities, but Mom and I would like it!"

"I'll run yer back, anyway," My dad had just been messing around with our car, taking some strange looking objects from the top of the cooker and carrying them back outside with a heavy duty glove.

"Sparkin' plugs!" Dave told us without being asked, from the depths of the other armchair.

"That's my brother!" I said, "Not goin' train spottin' with Roy today then, our kid?"

Dave yawned and stretched. "Nah — Lope's in the football team now — I'm gettin' a trial next wick!"

"'E's at the grammar school," I said, as Mom came back with cups of tea on a tray. "God 'elp 'em!"

Sally looked at Dave again. But if she was surprised, she didn't show it. "He must be clever, then," she said.

Though Dave squirmed, and later went out, saying he was going to Auntie May's to call for John, I could tell he was pleased. As for Mom, she acted as if my new friend had given her a fortune, just by praising her son.

"I'll just go and see to the dinner," she said, as she handed us a plate of "Nice" biscuits, to go with the tea. "It's sausage an' mash — if that's all right."

"Smashing!" Sally said, and as Mom disappeared, tying her apron more firmly around her still slim waist, her brown eyes met mine. "Your family's really nice, Carol," she said, "And I love your house!"

Remembering where she came from, I wondered how she could possibly mean the words, but she genuinely did seem to enjoy the meal and afterwards encouraged both Mom and Dad to join in the laughter when the two of us talked about the "Limes".

"Have you told them about the tuck shop being out of bounds, Carol?" she asked, and when I shook my head. "Y'see, the nearest place you can get sweets and crisps and things is this little shop round the back of the school, in Brunswick Park Road, but a few years ago, Mr. Donithorne made it out of bounds because of the dangers of us crossing the road . . ."

"Yes," I put in, encouraged by the way both my parents were listening. "but it's still the tuck shop because when the bell goes for break, the old lady from the shop, Mrs. Moore, crosses the road with a big cardboard box full of Spangles and toffee bars an' so on — an' the kids pass their money down, over the school wall!"

Sally grinned, as she smoothed back her hair. "The great thing is, Mr. Donnithorne knows it goes on, but he doesn't say anything," she said, "He told my dad went I went for my exam interview that he admires initiative, and one of the "Limes" kids must've shouted over the wall, until Mrs. Moore got the idea!"

She broke off, frowning in my direction as she took the last but one of the left over biscuits. "I go most days for my Rowntrees fruit gums," she said, "but I don't think I've seen you on the wall, Carol."

"N-no," I said hastily, picking up plates and taking them to the sink. "I us'ully take somethin' for break — an' besides, yer sometimes 'ave to wait too long, specially when 'er box gets empty an' people keep 'er on, goin' back an' forth!"

Lovely though she was, I didn't think Sally would quite understand that though we were marginally better off that when we lived in the Lost City estate, there were still days when my mother wouldn't have been able to provide money for sweets or crisps at break time.

In the middle of the afternoon, Sally said she'd promised to telephone her mom and dad. "Just to let them know when to expect me back," she said.

"You got a phone in yer 'ouse, then?" Dave, back with cousin John, looked at her with wide eyes. Though I pulled a face at him, I was secretly just as impressed.

"There's a phone box up on the terrace," I said, picking up our school macks and handing Sally hers. "Let's go an' try to get through on that!"

The workings of the local phone box were a mystery to me, but Sally had no trouble with buttons A and B, and was soon talking to her mother. Feeling awkward, I went outside to wait, and at the same moment, a figure skidded to a halt beside me. Joan on a bike!

"Thought yo couldn't ride one?" I asked, taken off guard, and she grinned triumphantly as she pushed her wind tousled hair out of her eyes.

"Learnt meself, day I?" she said, "One — two — three! It ay mine, anyway, it's me cousin's!" Then her attention was caught by the figure in the phone box. 'Oo's that? Is 'er with yo?"

"Yep!" I nodded as the heavy door opened and Sally came out. "I told Mom your dad was driving me home around six," she was saying, and then, seeing Joan. "Hello, I'm Sally. What's your name?"

Joan peered at her over the handlebars of the scratched red bike. Her jaw dropped open, and out of the side of it, she mouthed one word: "Posh!"

Then, after hastily wiping her nose on her sleeve, she said, grandly, "Hellooo, Sally! My name's Joan 'all! You may 'ave heard of my brother!"

"It ay really lies, it's like yer say — it's imagination!" Nan said, when I called in there for egg and chips one night after school and told her all about Joan and her notions of having a famous band leader in the family. "From what yow tell me about that little wench, 'er just needs somebody to gi' 'er a bit o' time — an' love!"

My nan was big on love, I reflected as I made my way back home along Powis Avenue and Summerhill. I grinned as I thought of her small, almost fierce face, telling me fervently: "These naughty boys who get in trouble an' get sent to them reproved schools — all they needed was somebody to love 'em when they was little! Nobody deserves to be locked up like that, an' they should on'y bring back 'angin' for them as murder policemen, or little old women like me!"

Being with Nan always gave me a new perspective on things, and I could even feel philosophical about not having a hula hoop.

"What'n they want to do that for?" she'd demanded, eyes blinking behind her glasses when I excitedly pointed out gyrating figures on her small t.v. screen. "It's enough ter dislocate yer blasted 'ips!"

As I dawdled on, pausing to buy chewing gum from a machine outside a shop, I told myself hula hoops were really for kids, anyway. I had other things to think about — like spending time writing the essays that Mr. Lynall was beginning to give me good marks for. And sitting by the radio, hoping they'd play a song by that sulky sounding young man from America called Elvis Presley.

My daydreams carried me — lifted me — all the way home so that I seemed to drift through the gate and along the side of the house, past the outside toilet and through the back door into the verandah. Then, I came, swiftly — painfully — back to earth.

"Where've yer' bin?" demanded my brother, his face white as chalk. "Mom wants yer!"

Frowning, I pushed past him into the living room, where to my shocked surprise, I found our mother lying on the sofa with a coat over her. Her face was twisted with pain and she gasped: "Go on, Dave! Fetch yer auntie May! Carol'll stop with me, now!"

As the door slammed behind Dave's flying figure, I dropped my satchel on the floor and fell to my knees beside Mom. "What is it, Mom?" I asked, my heart beating fast. "What c'n I do?"

Mom reached out her hand and touched my face as the spasm of pain passed. "It's all right, cock, yer cor do anythin'," she said, swallowing. "Our May'll know what to do if this is what I think . . ."

I bit my lip, wishing suddenly Dad was here, but he'd be on his way to work by now.

"What is it?" I asked again. In answer, Mom gritted her teeth and gripped my hand.

"It's what they call a "mis'," she whispered, as the tears filled and then gushed from both our eyes. "It means I'm losin' the babby!"

CHAPTER
SIXTEEN

"Que sera sera," sang Alma Coggan on "Family Favourites", "Whatever will be, will be!" Though none of us said so, it was our song for Victoria. Or Nicholas.

The weeks went by, and Mom gradually recovered, at least physically. "The doctor tode me it was what they call an ectopic pregnancy," she told me quietly one day when we were on our own. "That means it was growin' in the wrong place — an' so we 'ad to lose it!"

That "we" reminded me of the nice things Sally had said about my famly and I felt swiftly ashamed of the secret yearnings I'd harboured not so long ago to be adopted, and therefore mysterious like she was.

While Dad brought Mom an extra bottle of Guinness a day, and Nan tried unsuccessfully to build her up with raw egg and sherry, I decided to try and cheer her up with accounts of funny or dramatic things that happened at school.

"An' then Mr. Postins screamed in the German class, 'Wass ist das?' an' everybody nearly jumped out of their skin!"

"Well, our French class really stinks now!" My brother put in, not to be outdone. When Mom went out of the room to fetch her cardigan, he finished triumphantly: "Lope an' me got fed up wi' the stink bombs — so we've nailed a kipper under Monsoower's chair!"

"— Er — won't be long till Christmas now, will it?" I said hastily as the door opened and our mother reappeared. She gave a deep sigh then bent to poke some life into the fire. "I ay really thought about it, this year, Carol," she said, "but yo'm right. Yo'll soon be breakin' up for yer 'olidays again!"

On the Monday night before the end of term, an unexpected knock came at the verandah door. It was Joan Hall, her face cleaner and more anxious than I'd ever seen it, and a letter clutched in her hand.

"Our mother's tode me to come an' see yer," she began, and I ushered her inside, "On'y we got this today — from the Country Commercial School!"

"County — yer nit!" I retorted before I could stop myself. "'Ow many green fields yow sid in Wednesbury?"

Joan shrugged and handed me the letter. "It says I've got in, anyway," she said, as she sat on the chair my mother patted at the verandah table. "Subject to intervoow — what's that mean?"

I gulped as I opened the much handled piece of paper. "It means yer go an' talk to Mr. Donnithorne, the 'ead master," I explained, "But you never even said yo'd done the exam!"

Joan had the grace to blush. "They put me in fer it at my school, ages agoo! But I day know that I wanted to be a grammar grub!"

As our eyes met, I knew that, like me, she was remembering our very first meeting, the day I started at the "Limes". It was only a few months ago, but so much seemed to have changed, since then.

"Anyroad, some on yer don't seem so bad," she went on. "That Sally was really nice, even though 'er's posh, an' I dow need to bother with Bar, 'oo was so nasty!"

"Barbara's started goin' round with some wenches from the fourth year, now," I reassured her, "An' if yow do get through the interview, yer can come on the bus with me an' my other friend, Janice."

"Our mother says, if I goo ter that school, I might even end up a seccyterry!" Joan nodded her thanks, and took a noisy slurp from one of the mugs of liberally sugared tea that Mom put in front of us, with the usual biscuits.

"That's right, some get to do shorthand 'an' typin'," I confirmed, "In fact, last wick, my class, 3Y, 'ad a practice at typin'. I forgot to tell yer about it, Mom."

Mom pushed her dark hair out of her eyes and sat down with her own hot drink while I described the typing room, with its black metal machines, with the keys blacked out.

"That's so yer can't look at 'em while yer type," I explained, "You 'ave to keep yer eyes on the wall, where there's a chart — with all the letters and numbers in front of yer. It's called 'touch typing' — an' we did it to music!"

"Music?" Joan nearly choked on the "morning coffee" she had dunked then slid whole into her mouth. "Yer mean like rock 'n' roll?"

"No! More like band music," I caught myself just as I was about to unwisely mention Henry Hall, and said, quickly: "The teacher, Mr. Miller, 'ad a wind up gramaphone an' one record 'Chicago' an' we was supposed to type to it."

"Chicago — Chicago — I know it!" Mom suddenly smiled, as she took a biscuit from the fast diminishing pile. "It's on the wireless ever such a lot!"

"An' did yer type to it?" Joan wanted to know.

I nodded over my steaming mug. "Ar — faster 'an faster — 'cos Mr. Miller got called out of the classroom an' Margaret Wilkins would the gramaphone up right to the top, so it was goin' like like — 'Chicago — Chicago — that toddlin' town' . . ."

Putting the mug down, I waved both arms in the air to mimic the manic sound and motion. Then, encouraged by the laughter of Mom and Joan, I demonstrated how by the time Mr. Miller came back to the class, the complete reverse was happening.

"It went like this — 'Chic-a-a-a-a-a-r-g-o! Chic-a-a-a-a-a-r-g-o!' An' we all typed along — one key about every five seconds!"

"Well, I 'on'y 'ope 'e tode yer all off!" Mom felt bound to say as with a reproving shake of her head, she began to clear the table. But I knew it wasn't what she really meant, at all.

Christmas came, bringing with it a bright red hula hoop that I couldn't make stay up even for as long as it took to say "hula hoop." In addition to my usual book, which this year was *A Tale of Two Cities*, Nan also gave me a "vanity" case — a blue handbag whose lid had a mirror on the other side — and I also got my first ever pair of nylon stockings.

The suspender belt that went with them felt very strange, and I had to really persevere to fasten the little rubberised buttons and metal holders. Mom had said to do it at the top, so that's what I did, and a moment later, saw to my horror and amazement, four matching ladders running straight down my legs!

"I meant fasten them in the double bit — not the nylon part with the pretty pattern!" Mom hit her forehead with her hand as Dad and Dave both roared with laughter. "So it looks like ankle socks for Auntie May's party, then!"

Since moving to Central Avenue, Auntie May's party had become an integral part of our Christmas. Her large brood all gathered in the family house in Ivy Road and the four of us were welcomed.

"Where's Susan?" Mom asked, as the two of us squashed together into one space on the already full sofa. I glanced at her uncertainly, but though her eyes filled with tears at the appearance of her baby niece, now beginning to toddle, she seemed to gain strength and comfort as she lifted her into her arms.

"Yo'm a little beauty!" she crooned, kissing her soft curls. And Susan responded by reaching up to pat Mom's face. "Da-da!" she said.

"'Er calls everybody that!" Uncle Tom grinned as he appeared with Dad, carrying a glass of Guinness. "'Ere, our Liza, get that down yer, my wench!"

As Mom put Susan down and took the drink, I got up and wandered into the kitchen where the table was groaning with Christmas food, and Auntie May was in the process of pouring glasses of fizzy pop for what seemed like a regiment of waiting children.

"Tizer or ice cream soda, our Carol?" she asked, as I joined the queue.

"Ice cream soda, please," I replied. Although I knew it didn't have ice cream in it, or even say it on the label, I liked the name. And that always made it taste like something special.

All too soon, Christmas was over and we were back at school with, for me at any rate, the pressure about those vital GCEs getting greater all the time. The positive side of this single-mindedness was that none of us would be required to continue with subjects we found impossible. In my case, those were German, Statistics and Science, while I excelled in English Language and Literature, Commerce and, to my own astonishment, also found myself quite capable at History.

This was due to the perseverence and dedication of our whirlwind history master Mr. Gilson who had told us in our first ever lesson that he intended every single one of us to gain an "O" level pass in Social and Economic History.

"Mr. Gilson's takin' we all on a walk on Saturday," I told the family one February evening as we lingered in the verandah over tea. "Apparantly, they've found this ode manor 'ouse in West Bromwich — with a moat an' everythin' — an' it's goin' to be turned into a public 'ouse!"

It was when I got back from the trek to the manor house that Mom told me some news.

"I'm goin' to look for an evenin' job, our Carol," she said, her face solemn and purposeful. "Yo'm nearly fourteen now, an' Dave's gettin' to be a big lad — big enough to be left fer a couple of 'ours!"

"But what about Dad?" I asked, glancing towards the side of the house where, as usual, he was out tinkering with the car. Over the years, I'd heard him say — and Mom relate to other people — that if she went out to work, he'd give his job up. It was something to do with a man's pride in being able to support his family!

Mom smiled and shook her head. "We've bin all through it since — since I lost the babby, an' 'e agrees with me that it'd be good for me to get out among other women. Now, our May's 'eard they'm settin' on a twilight shift at the Champion bakery in Dudley!"

She sighed as she looked around the verandah that meant so much to her. I remembered the times recently she'd dreamt aloud of filling its spaces with a twintub washer, a formica dining set and the very latest in sink units.

"I never 'ad much when I was a kid — bein' brought up by Granny Coley — scrimpin' an' scrapin' — aving to wear other folks' cast offs!" she said, almost to herself. "I want you an' our Dave to 'ave what I never did! If I get a little job, we'll be able to goo out more — to the pictures or out in the country in the car. It'll be a new start for all on we!"

EPILOGUE

That Saturday night, we went for a ride "in the country" meeting Nan and Grandad in their car, at the carpark of the "New Inn" at Wallheath. It was a mild, spring evening, warm enough to "walk out" as Mom always rather grandly put it, in a cardigan and cotton dress. And I revelled in the fact that I wore unladdered nylon stockings under mine.

Dave and I watched as the grown ups climbed eagerly out of the two cars and made their way into the bar. They had no qualms about setting us down here, where lots of other kids chased around and we could get some fresh air while they had a drink, a chat and a sing song.

Sitting on a low wall a few yards from the "outdoor" we waited until Dad came out with two bottles of Vimto and two packets of Smiths crisps. "Mek 'em last!" he warned, before going back inside. "I dow want to be back an' forth all night . . ."

"Like a parched pae!" My brother finished, as he poked his straw up and down to make the Vimto fizz. Opening my crisps, I leant my back against the wall. Through the open window a few yards away, I could see the back of Mom and Nan's heads and I knew they would be sipping stout — a Guinness for Mom and a "Macky" for Nan. While on the other side of the table, Dad and Grandad enjoyed their "drap of Banks" beer.

"Finished!" Dave triumphantly drained his Vimto, having impatiently got rid of the straw, and let out a series of impressive burbs. Then, he tore open his crisps, and made them disappear, too.

Two bottles of Vimto and packets of delicious "Nibbits" later, Dad, red in the face, called "Time!"

"Don't you dare knock the winder again!" he told us both vehemently. "It's frightnin' the ode ladies an' purrin we all off we beer!"

Rapping on the open window when our supplies had gone had seemed like a good idea at the time, and Dave and I had taken it in turns to get the family's attention, holding up our bottles as a signal as Mom's head twisted round, and Nan automatically clutched her throat.

"We'm comin' out soon!" Mom had now joined Dad, her face somehow managing to be both exasperated and tender in the fading light. Since she'd been working at the "Champion" bakery, she had lost her gaunt look, thanks mainly to the half price broken cakes she was able to bring home for our threesome suppers.

"Dun yer want to wait in the car?" she offered, and then, turning to Dad. "Open it up for 'em, 'Arold!"

Obviously dubious about this suggestion, Dad never the less complied, giving us dire warnings, to "stay in the back" and on no account to touch anything!

It was warm and dark on the slippery back seat, and I soon began to feel sleepy.

"D'yer remember," I yawned, "The time we went to Hampton Loade — an' yo' climbed that big tree when they was in the pub — an' ripped yer trousers when yer fell out?"

"Right into that great pile o' cowshit!" Gleefully, Dave supplied the details, though he too was sounding drowsy.

"An' me dad said — trust yo' to find it!"

"Wum!" we both said together as we relived the horror, and the unwitting hilarity of the long ago, grown up fury, "BLOODY WUM!"

In spite of everything, there was still no better place to be!

A WOODBINE ON
THE WALL

CHAPTER
ONE

"Oh, well done, Carol!" beamed Mfanwy Jones, the games mistress. "You went round the course in ten minutes this time!"

Ignoring the smirk on the face of my best friend Sheila, I took another long and shuddering breath and leant against the nearest copper beech tree. As its branches shaded me from Mfanwy's proud gaze, I wondered what she would say if she knew that far from running our hearts out round the "Limes" cross country run course, Sheila and I had just spent the last ten minutes sitting on a wall outside St Paul's church. Sharing a Woodbine cigarette.

It had all started months before, when Sheila and I, sitting hating hockey with all the sulleness of lumpy 15-year olds, had noticed that in every games lesson, one or two other girls were "excused" and allowed to trot off the through the school gates.

"They can't be 'unwell' every week," Sheila had commented, reminding us both of the many times we two had used this particular ploy since becoming best friends in year 4. And so I'd put up my hand and asked the sweetly energetic games mistress, "Miss? Where'm they gooin'?"

Mfanwy turned and looked at me, obviously surprised at my sudden interest. "Where are they going, Carol," she repeated, airily. "Diction, dear, diction! Why — Pamela and Celia are off to practise for the cross country run! It happens every year at Sports Day!"

The mere mention of Sports Day was enough to turn Sheila's smirk into a shudder. Like me, she'd much rather be reading than exercising. Unless of course the exercise was jiving in the girls' cloakroom as we sang the songs of Buddy Holly.

"Could we go an' practise, Miss?" Ignoring Sheila's horrified stare, I'd jumped to my feet, briskly straightening my regulation blue aertex shirt and pushing it into the baggy navy blue shorts. "We'm both good runners, ay we, Sheil?"

"First I've 'eard on it!" mumbled my friend as the games mistress, blowing her whistle to control our eager, hockey stick wielding classmates, fairly jumped up and down with excitement. "Where we goin', Carol? 'ave yer gone saft?"

"Out through the gates ..." Mfanwy, whistle dangling over her cosy fur coat, gesticulated towards the crumbling stone walls of the "Limes." "Turn left, then right, into St Paul's Close, then past the church, and along Woden Road East, under the bridge and back to school! Off you go, girls — and I'll be timing you!"

Now, the teacher pocketed her stopwatch and told us benignly. "Ten minutes was your best time ever! I think you'd better go back to the changing rooms now and rest!"

Sheila and I didn't need telling twice. Clutching non-existent stitches in our sides, pretending to fight for every breath, we limped past the girls who were still playing hockey.

By the time they crowded into the tiny changing rooms, Sheila and I were back in our school uniforms, the hated games kit stowed away in our navy blue pump bags for another week.

"Hey?" asked Janice Smith, who I travelled on the bus with each day. Her face was pink from her exertions. "'Ow come yow two get out of games all the time now?"

At 15, Janice was tall and slim, her plaits long discarded in favour of a more fashionable Peter Pan haircut.

"We don't!" I protested, as Sheila offered me a tablet of Beech Nut spearmint and I popped it in my mouth. "We go practisin'!"

"Ar — smokin' an' swiggin' school milk on the church wall!" Sharp Barbara Phipps put in as she sat down in a cloud of Body Mist anti-perspirant. "My mother sid yer last wick, when 'er come past on the bus!"

"Well, anyroad . . ." Sheila coughed loudly as the crowd near the door parted and Mfanwy Jones sailed in. Her eyes bright and encouraging beneath her tousled fair hair, the games mistress looked quickly around.

"Ah — Carol — Sheila!" she said, self importantly pulling a piece of paper out of her pocket, "Before you go off to your next lesson. Mr. Donithorne has just given me the date for this year's Sports Day — and it's not too far away! Now, of course I'll be putting you two girls down to take part in the cross country run!"

"Serves yer right!" said my mother when I told her grumpily that Sheila and I now had to prove our non existent prowess at running in front of the whole school. "Yer know what they say — 'be sure your sins'll find you out'!"

I shifted a bit guiltily under her green gaze, remembering the shared Woodbine that I knew she'd see as an even greater sin.

"Anyroadup," she went on briskly as she picked up her gondolier-shaped wicker basket and prepared to go off to work. "Yo pair just be'ave yerselves while I'm away!"

Wiry, and small for his thirteen years, my brother Dave merely nodded. He seemed very quiet and preoccupied as he sprawled in front of the fire. Dragging my duffle bag of books behind me, I went slowly up the narrow staircase to my bedroom at the back of the house. As always, it felt icily cold — a reminder of how far away it was from the living room with its coal-burning grate.

To write my English Literature essay homework, I knew I'd end up keeping on my school mack and the gloves my nan still knitted me every Christmas, and I usually lost by February.

But the house, especially the upper storey, was quiet, and as I sat on the bed and took out my books, an air of both calm and ease came over me. The book we were studying at the moment was *The History of Mr. Polly* by H. G. Wells and I took the borrowed school text out of my bag and began to read the relevant pages.

The passage was all about Christabel, the beautiful young woman Mr. Polly met on his bicycle rides into the countryside. She had long, red hair, and she sat on the top of a wall, on the other side of which was a school.

Closing my eyes, I could almost smell the trees overhanging the wall — could feel the warmth of the sun even though it was cold and rather uncomfortable in the January bedroom — a place not designed for study at all.

It all reminded me of that poem I'd learnt by heart after Mr. Lynall read it to us last year. The poem all about the donkey, Nicholas Nye.

"Thistle and darnell and dock grew there —
And a bush in the corner, of may . . ."

Suddenly even more aware of the cold, I got up and paced up and down, saying the words aloud in a monologue of delight at just the sound of them:

"On the orchard wall, where I used to sprawl
In the dying heat of the day . . ."

"Oo yer talkin' to?" I nearly dropped dead with fright when my brother appeared suddenly in the now open doorway. "I think yo've gone saft!" he went on, automatically picking things up from my dressing table and putting them down again. "What's this blue stuff for?"

"Eye shadow!" I snatched it off him and put it safely in my pocket. There was still something about him I couldn't put my finger on, and I wondered if he were in any trouble at school. "Leave me alone, I'm doin' me writin'!" I told him. "What yer want, anyway?"

"Nothin'!" he replied, infuriatingly, and then, from halfway down the stairs. "Smelly Joan's just called for yer, that's all!"

Joan Hall stood waiting by the verandah door. As usual, her grey socks were at half mast and it looked as if she hadn't combed her hair for a week. "Lo, Carol," she said, through a mouthful of pink bubble gum. "Comin' out?"

With one eye on my brother, who was holding his nose in a corner of the living room, I told her quickly that I had to stay in till our mother got back. "But you can come in," I offered triumphantly as Dave moaned out loud. "Tek no notice of 'im! Come an' tell me all the news. We'll sit by the fire!"

Beaming, Joan took up the seat opposite me. Since starting at the "Limes'" nearly two years ago now, she'd had lots to talk about, mainly about the antics of her classmates.

"Them Thomsons twins is bloody snobs, ay they?" she began, stretching the gum in and out of her mouth. "One on 'em — Marcella — that fat 'un — 'ad the cheek to tell me to get me skirt washed last wick! It's on'y cos 'er was jealous cos I always come top in maths!"

"You'll prob'ly get a prize for that, yer know," I replied, amazed that anyone — let alone Joan Hall — could — ever — come top in maths. "Remember last year — at speech day?"

Joan's pale blue eys opened wide. "I cor imagine our mother or dad comin' to that," she said, "but me brother 'Enry 'All might, if 'e ay too busy playin' in 'is band!"

After Joan had gone, trailing down the street like a miniature ghost, I looked at the clock and got up the put the kettle on.

"Mom'll be back soon," I told my brother. "Mek the fire up, will yer?"

He usually complained, but tonight, to my surprise, he went into the coal-house and came back with a bucket of small coal which he threw on the back of the fire. Then, he followed me back into the verandah and stood watching as I got the mugs out, ready for cocoa.

For a long moment, he said nothing, and then out it came, all in a rush, "Our Carol, some of the lads've bin talkin' — an' I day know what they was on about . . ."

"Oh?" I turned and frowned, beginning to feel uncomfortable without knowing why. "What was they sayin'?"

Dave studiously avoided my eyes, his toe digging into the coconut mat. "About wenches," he mumbled. "An' summat that 'appens to 'em every month . . . !"

"Oh!" I swallowed, the discomfort settling immediately into hot embarrassment.

"I dunno!" I said, with a quick laugh, and as the lie floated transparently between us, "Look — Mom'll be in soon. Yer can ask 'er!"

A look of sheer horror passed over my brother's face. "I cor do that! 'Er'll think I'm rude!" he said, the unfamiliar word flooding his face with even deeper colour. "Yo tell me, our Carol — it wo' 'urt yer!"

"Oh — all right then!" Rattling the mugs, I prepared to mumble the few facts I'd discovered for myself through personal experience. "Yer won't like it, though!" I warned, and as stunned disbelief gradually joined the horror on his face, I saw with some satisfaction that I was right!

CHAPTER
TWO

"There!" With a satisfied gleam in her eye, Nan pulled the yards of blue and white gingham from under the levers of her old sewing machine and quickly reached for her scissors.

"Never forget to tie off the ends, our Carol!" she advised me as her small, deft fingers made knots in the trailing white thread. "Otherwise, yo'll all come unravelled . . ."

"Okay, Nan." My own fingers itched to get at the new skirt into which I'd persuaded her to gather a whole three yards of remnant material. "C'n I try it on now?"

Stepping out of my baggy school skirt, I pulled the blue and white confection up over my hips. All it needed, I thought longingly, was one of those big net underskirts and it would stick out all around me in that way that was all the fashion!

"'Ooks an' eyes an' press-studs . . ." Nan's mind was obviously on more practical matters as she bent her white head over the old biscuit tin where she kept her store of sewing requisites. "Best put both on — yo' bein' such a rant-all!"

"I ay!" I protested before I realised she was joking. By the time I saw the skirt again, I knew it would be complete, every stray cotton removed, each fastening sewn on to withstand even the roughest treatment. Pressed and aired, it would be hung in the back bedroom, waiting for me to collect it.

There was an added bounce to my step as I practised jiving with Sheila in the girls' cloakroom next day, and I told her, "My nan's mekking me this lovely bopping skirt — then I'm gonna start goin' to the Con dance on Friday nights! They play all the latest records!"

Sheila concentrated on twirling me under her arm. It was hard without music, but we never gave up and today it was our favourite Everly brothers hit that we sang.

"All I have to do is — dre — ee — ee — ee — m — dream dream dream!"

"They play em at Brownhills dance hall where I go," she said. "Pity you live so far away — we could go dancin' together!"

I did another little twirl, narrowly missing tall, bespectacled Margaret Turner, who was politely trying to get to the sink. I didn't even know if my mom and dad would let me go to the nearest dance hall, and even though I had the skirt, there were still the boppers, the top and the all important underskirt needed!

"My gran used to be a dancer, you know, Carol." Margaret's quiet voice seemed to come from nowhere. I blinked across to where she was standing, half looking

212

at our awkwardly determined movements. "She was on the stage — and in lots of shows," she said.

To show how unimpressed she was, Sheila gave an impressive shrug. Somehow, our hands had dropped and we were no longer jiving. "Not doin' rock 'n' roll she wasn't!" she said, moving past the hovering Margaret to readjust her backcombed hair. "That slow-slow-quick-quick-slow stuff's so square!"

I agreed, but I still couldn't help but be intrigued. As the bell sounded and we began to trail towards our next classroom, and Commerce, I stared after Margaret, who was clever enough to be taking Science.

When I was a little girl, living on the Lost City estate, I'd dreamt of being discovered by Carroll Levis — both singing and dancing. What must it have been like, I wondered, as Commerce began and seemed to go on forever, to be on the stage, and in shows?

It seemed I'd soon get the chance to find out because when Janice, Joan and I went out to get our bus, Margaret was waiting to speak to me again.

"If you want to meet my gran, I'll take you on Saturday! You can come to my 'ouse for your dinner, if you like!"

She smiled, her eyes looking very big and hopeful behind her pink plastic glasses. Surprised and flattered, I nodded. "Thanks, Margaret. I'll come — if it's all right with yer mom."

Margaret nodded firmly as she put on her school beret and belted her mack. Unlike most of us, she still carried a satchel and it was obviously full of books. "We like to 'ave visitors," she said. "Me brothers'll be really pleased, an' all!"

"Ooh, brothers, eh?" chorused Joan and Janice, nudging me as Margaret hurried on her way. "Wonder what they'm like!"

Speculations ranging from Billy Fury to Tommy Steele and back again lasted until we were on the bus and headed back to Tipton.

"Tell yer what though, Carol," Janice finally said, thoughtfully. "Margaret's really doin' well at school. Me mate's in 5S an' 'er says Margaret comes top in nearly everythin'! I reckon er'll stop on an' do "A" levels."

"Or even go to the Universe!" We both turned and stared as Joan, removing her beret to scratch her tousled head, tutted from one to the other of us. "Yo know — that Oxford plerce Mr. Gilson's always on about! Margaret might end up goin' there!"

The following Saturday morning, I got up early and caught the bus into Dudley, where Margaret and I had arranged to meet. It was a cold January day, but I couldn't resist wearing my new gingham skirt.

"You look really nice, Carol," Margaret said, shyly, as she walked up to me in her familiar school mack. "I like the way you've got your cardigan!"

I smiled, her admiration making me momentarily forget my shivers. The voice of Mom telling me I was sure to catch my "jeth!" faded out of my recent memory as I said, "I couldn't find a top to go wi' me new dancin' skirt, so I thought I'd wear me school cardi done up backwards!"

"Very nice," said Margaret, squinting slightly at the cardigan's label, its wobbly angle by my neck. "Er — we can walk to my 'ouse from 'ere. I know a short cut.!"

The short cut seemed very long to me, past factories and down back alleys where there was no trace of even a blade of grass. But we passed the time in talking about school, and friends, and interests.

"I like history," Margaret said, unexpectedly, as we turned the corner into a street of sand-coloured council houses. "You know — how people used to live, an' all that. I've read loads of books about it!"

I nodded, wondering a little uncomfortably if Margaret's family would be all studious, too. My mind went back, of its own volition, to my days at St Mark's C. of E. junior school, where I had always felt inferior to the middle class favourites, Mary Gregory and Pamela Simms. Perhaps for all her apparent warmth and friendliness, Margaret was "one of them"!

"Here it is." I was soon following her down the path of one of the houses towards an open front door. A plump woman in a floral pinafore stood inside beaming, a curly haired baby on her hip and two small boys standing one each side.

"This is my mom, an' these am my brothers, Joey, Alan an' Michael — e's the baby." Margaret introduced almost formally. "This is Carol — from school."

"Pleased to meet yer, Carol." Margaret's mom released her hold on Michael long enough to shake my hand. "Take Carol inside, love," she said, gently, to

Margaret. "Gordon and Desmond are inside, with yer dad."

"More brothers!" Margaret explained. She raised her eyebrows before leading me into the living room. A fire burnt brightly behind a big mesh fire-guard, there was a worn three piece suite, a sideboard, television and a table in the bay window which was already laid with plates and cups and saucers.

While Margaret introduced me to her dad, a tall man with thinning hair and spectacles, the younger of her other two brothers, Desmond, edged over and shyly reached up for my hand. "Lo," he said. "What's your name?"

I looked down into an angelic face framed with long auburn curls. After telling him my name I found out that he was four years old and wanted nothing more in life than to sit at my side at the dinner table and chatter!

"Our Gordon's quite independent," Mrs Turner said, nodding to the other, quieter small boy who sat down next to his sister "but Desmond's obviously fallen in love with you!" Efficiently, she handed the baby to Margaret, installed the toddlers one each side of their father and then disappeared into the kitchen.

"It's only bacon an' egg, Carol," she apologised, coming back with plates a few moments later, "But there's plenty of bread, an' we can wash it down with lots of tea!"

Over the simple meal, I found myself relaxing and really enjoying the company of Margaret and her family. "We had quite a shock when our Margy passed

216

for the Commercial," her dad said, suddenly, " 'er bein' the eldest, an' the only girl, like!"

I nodded, thinking of the struggle my own, smaller family had had. "I've just got one brother, two years younger than me," I explained, "Me mom was 'avin "another baby, but she 'ad a 'miss' . . ." I looked down at Desmond with his cheek on my arm and felt a sudden pang for the not-to-be baby whom we'd called Nicholas or Victoria.

"Just be thankful you ay got five brothers!" Margaret said, into a barrage of roaring protest. Then she turned to her mom and grinned. "Shall I go an' fetch the fruit cake in, Mom?"

After lunch was cleared away, all Margaret's brothers settled on the floor around the television set, except Desmond, who was squashed into the space between me and the armchair.

"Shall we go an' see my gran now?" Margaret suggested as the mantlepiece clock struck two. "She's expectin' us!"

Margaret's gran lived in a prefab two streets away. Leaving Desmond to squat, sighing, between the toddlers on the hearth rug, we took the small parcel Mrs Turner wordlessly handed over the baby's head and left while it was quiet.

"Come on in, me luvvers!" The old lady was as round as she was high, with grey hair done in a bun and bird bright brown eyes. "Tek no notice of the parrot!" she instructed, as she led us past a cage with a loudly squawking bright bird in it. " 'e goes mad when I 'as company!"

In the tiny living room, Margaret and I sat opposite her gran on the sofa. It was warm in there, but she was wearing two jumpers and a brightly coloured woollen shawl.

"So yo'm our Margy's friend from that posh school in Wensbry?" she said, and as I nodded and began to tell her my name, "Never 'ad much eddication meself, I was an exotic dancer, yer know . . ."

Raising her several chins, she nodded to the wall near the door, where for the first time, I saw a glass-fronted photograph. Two big men in leotards, and between them, a tiny little creature in a spangled costume and feathered head-dress.

Intrigued, I stood up and went to the picture. "They chucked me from one to the other, right across the stage," the old lady explained, obviously pleased by my interest. "Really summat, it was — ter see me fly through the air!"

As I stared at the fascinating old photo, Margaret's voice seemed to come from another dimension. "Mom's sent yer some fruit cake, Gran . . ."

"But how . . .?" I looked from the sparrow-like creature in front of me to the rotundly contented little woman in the armchair.

Margaret's gran shuddered, then took a huge grateful bite out of the unwrapped cake. "Easy, cock," she said. "They bloody clammed me, day they?"

CHAPTER
THREE

A factory "bull" sounded, echoeing along Central Avenue from the other side of the Cracker, a working quarry that always reminded me of an eerie landscape from another galaxy.

The animal-like call demanded that sleeping or dawdling workers make their way to one of the many Tipton foundries. Maybe the one where my Uncle Tom had worked until his premature death, twelve months ago.

If I got out of bed and looked through the front window, I knew I'd see a street full of movement as people of all ages and both sexes hurried to answer the call and put in the time that would eventually bring in Friday night, and a pay packet.

"Yo'll just 'ave to save up yer pocket money for the things yo want, my wench!" My mother's oft repeated words came back to me as I sat up and automatically reached for the book I'd placed on the lino before falling asleep the night before. "By the time I was your age, I was workin' — doin' ten hours a day in a french polishin' shop!"

I sighed as I opened *The History of Mr Polly* again, wondering what it must be like to actually go out to work like most of my cousins, Auntie May's children. Anne and John both thought it strange, I knew, that I was stopping on at school to the age of sixteen. Though Mr. Donithorne, our headmaster stressed daily the importance of taking our GCEs, there were times, like now, that I wondered.

" 'Ow'm I gonna get the boppers — they'm 12s and 11 pence!" I complained to Sheila next time we sat on the wall of St. Paul's church, courtesy of Mfanway's stopwatch. "I on'y get a shillin' a week pocket money — an' then there's the underskirt!"

"I'm gettin' my underskirt with a Provident cheque!" my best friend told me cheerfully as she watched me swig at the bottle of milk we'd picked up from the crate by the canteen wall. We didn't have a Woodbine today, but it was perhaps as well if Barbara Phipp's nosey mother was likely to come past on the bus!

I shivered in the January air and stamped my feet in their hated school plimsolls. "I wonder if I could ave an underskirt with a cheque as well," I pondered wistfully. 'Ow much do they cost, Sheil?"

"FIVE POUNDS?" My mother's eyes widened with sheer astonishment as I mumbled my request over the verandah table that evening. "Fer a bit o' lace an' starched netting. That's 'alf a wick's wages!"

"You on'y pay five bob a week back on the cheque," I was conscious that Nan too was staring at me, her face very stern over the shopping bag on her knee.

"Yo cor just goo inter debt like that, our Carol!" she admonished, as Mom nodded over the plates and

220

cutlery. "Why, I bet I could run yer up one o' them fancy petticoats out of a couple o' yards o' net curtain off Great Bridge market!"

Looking at her suddenly excited face, my heart sank with a mixture of dismay and guilt that was suddenly hard to bear. I thought of my shiny school blouses with their homemade name tags

"It's all right, Mom." Surprised, I saw my own mother looking from one to the other of us, and seeming to come to a decision. "I'll sort it out," she went on quickly. "Now let's get that neck o' lamb down we afore it all goes cold!"

Next day at school, I told Sheila uncertainly what Mom had said, and then went and sat in top of the school wall with Joan. Like me, she enjoyed watching the progress of Mrs. Moore from the out of bounds sweet shop across the road. At break, and again at lunch time, she would trot across to the "Limes" with a laden cardboard box of goodies for pupils to buy over the back wall.

"Er must be good at maths," Joan said, thoughtfully, as she absently gnawed at her bitten down finger nails. "I dunno 'ow 'er remembers the prices of all them suck — an' 'er reckons up the change really fast!"

"Ar." I nodded, the sixpence I had burning a hole in my pocket. Remembering the warning I'd had about saving, I calculated that if I kept it, I'd only have to scrape up just over twelve shillings for the essential boppers. It might as well have been twelve hundred pounds.

"'Ere, let's 'ave a Mars bar!" I decided, as Joan's face lit up beside me. "I'll just pass down the tanner, then we can break the suck in 'alf!"

"Let's climb up 'ere to 'ave it!" Joan suggested a few moment's later as I finished dividing the sweet into two equal halves. As the remaining pupils crowded round the busy shopkeeper, she led me down the wall to where it met an outhouse roof. "Yo can see the lads coming from the 'igh school from 'ere!" she said, as she clambered like a monkey up the slope.

Joining her, I saw that the view took in almost the whole of Brunswick Park Road. To add to the adventure, there was also a huge, shady tree which overhung the outhouse roof and made us seem invisible.

"This is nice!" I said as I bit into the soft toffee and chocolate. The pavement below the wall looked far off and the sounds of the school could have been coming from another world.

Trying to get higher into the branches of the tree, I somehow got my left leg trapped underneath me, and as I struggled, my ugly school shoe suddenly slipped off my right foot and fell like a stone towards the pavement.

"Oh no!" I said, pushing the last of the Mars bar into my mouth while Joan gawped. At the same time, to my astonished embarrassment, the sound of male voices came from the pavement below. "Hey — where's that come from?"

Looking through the branches, I saw, upturned, a boy's face, fresh and good looking, beneath a mop of

222

fair hair. He was about 15, and like the other two boys at his side, wore the uniform of Wednesbury Boys High School.

"It — it's my shoe!" I hissed, unnecessarily as Joan began to chortle delightedly at my side. "But we cor — can't — go out!"

As the boy frowned, still holding the shoe, my heart gave an unexpected thud. It was just like Mr. Polly and Christabel, I thought, romantically. All that was missing was the bicycle!

A moment later, I was startled out of my day dreams by the fact that the school bell was ringing, and the other two boys had somehow got hold of the shoe and were throwing it from one to the other:

'Ere, Terry — catch!"

"See if yer can throw it up to 'er, Mick!"

I leant over, trying unsuccessfully to catch the flying shoe, and for a split second, the fair haired boy looked straight at me and grinned. Then, two things happened at once. The bell rang again to say afternoon lessons were about to begin, and my dream boy caught the shoe!

For one split second, I felt like Cinderella. And then, amid guffaws, Prince Charming raised my clumsy school footwear to his nose. said, "Poo!" in a very loud and meaningful way. Then he flung the shoe at full tilt right over the wall and into the middle of the playground!

"E must like yer, Carol!" Joan reasoned, puzzlingly, as, cheeks burning in mortification, I readjusted my dress and almost ran in the direction of my English class. "I bet 'e'll come round tomorrow to see if yo'll do it again!"

"E needn't bother!" I muttered, as Joan waved and disappeared into her Statistics class. I vowed to keep well away from the school wall in future, and to keep my Mars bar money in my pocket!

The following Friday I got home to find Mom waiting, her face wreathed in smiles. Usually, she had to dash off to her twilight shift at the bakery, but today she seemed to have more time.

"Yer dad's drivin' me, as 'e's off tonight," she explained, adjusting her softly curled dark hair through the mantelpiece mirror. "Then 'e's pickin' me up an we'm poppin' out for a drink. But before we goo, I want yer to go up an' look in yer bedroom."

"Me?" I hesitated, and she gave me a little nudge. "Go on — it's a surprise!"

Running up the stairs two at a time, I flung open my bedroom door. There, on the bed, to my astonishment and delight, was a three-tiered nylon and net white underskirt, exactly right for rock 'n' roll!

"Like it?" Mom beamed. "I got a bonus comin' this wick, so I thought I'd treat yer!"

I grabbed the underskirt, too thrilled to speak. "Oh Mom, it's great — thanks!" I finally burst out, as I flew into her arms.

She held me for just a moment and I knew that through her pleasure at giving me the gift there was, as always, the memory of sadness because at my age, she'd had so few pretty things.

"Try it on with your checked skirt," she said, "An' next time I go into Wednesbury, I'll get yer a pair o' them boppers to go with it!"

CHAPTER
FOUR

"One — two — three o' clock, four o' clock rock!"

The music belted out of the record player on the dance hall stage, and Janice Smith and I just stood there looking at each other.

"Don't forget we've gorra catch the ten o' clock bus, Carol!" she whispered nervously, as a group of girls pushed past us and began bopping in twos on the edge of the floor. "Or me dad wo' let me come again!"

I nodded as I adjusted the itchy edges of my back to front school cardigan. I looked at Janice in her best white blouse and scotch plaid kilt and wished guiltily that my first time at the "Con" could've been with Sheila, instead. But Sheila lived on the other side of Brownhills, at a far off place called Clayhanger. And the only way I'd been able to persuade my parents to let me out was to promise to stay in a twosome with Janice, who had the advantage of living in the same street as me.

As the music seemed to swell and reverberate round the walls, I felt my spirits rise. "Come on," I said to Janice. "Let's bop!"

Small and light on her feet, she was soon twirling around while I tried to catch and swing her under my arm. It was so hypnotic that I scarcely noticed when the floor began to fill up and the music changed.

This was what I had been dreaming about for what seemed like years — the opportunity to move to the new and exciting songs that put into words all the things that couldn't be expressed in any other way.

I looked around and realised that apart from the middle-aged man operating the record player and his mate who had taken our two shillings at the door, everyone here was young and free and absolutely ready for whatever the phenomena of rock and roll was bringing into their lives. It was the headiest feeling I'd ever known!

"It's stopping!" Her anxiety forgotten, Janice wiped the perspiration from her face and nodded to where the man on the stage was taking the last record off. "Interval!" he announced, and there was a mass stampede for the door!

Linking arms, Janice and I followed curiously at a distance and saw that in the corridor the doorman was now selling bottles of pop, while the man who had turned the records was issueing pieces of paper to an impatient queue of couples by the door.

"I've 'eard o' them!" Janice told me, eyes wide with disapproval. "They'm passouts! They go outside an' snog round the back o' the 'all!"

"Oh?" Wishing I had something cooler to dance in than the dark woolly cardigan, I was more interested in the other queue. "Wonder 'ow much the Vimto is?"

After the interval, the "Con" really seemed to fill up, so that there was scarcely room to dance.

"Watch it!" growled a tough looking girl, jiving with a boy in a draped coat and crêpe soled shoes and I realised too late I'd bumped into her, making her teeter momentarily on her white, stiletto heeled shoes.

"S-sorry!" I mumbled, and managed to steer Janice away towards the centre of the now gyrating mob of youngsters. Though I was scared, I was exhilarated, too! A dance hall was a dangerous as well as an exciting place to be!

Janice and I bopped until we could bop no more, and I was already planning what I'd be telling Sheila about it at school on Monday morning when the strains of Little Richard suddenly stopped belting out from the stage.

Everyone stopped dead, then, to my surprise, began to regroup into couples. The lights were dimmed, a dreamy ballad began to play, and a whisper went round, "Creeps!"

"Do you want to dance?" I turned at the voice at my side and in the half light, saw a boy in a flecked tweed jacket. He was about average height and his mouth curled into a shyly hopeful smile beneath a quiff of thick brown curls.

Surprised, I nodded and he moved towards me, holding his hands as if for a formal waltz. I let him take my hand and hold my waist, while at the same time, Janice was led off by another boy who again seemed to have appeared from nowhere.

While the strains of "Only Make Believe" rang in my ears, I looked over my partner's shoulder and saw couples moving closer, heads on shoulders, lips meeting in lingering kisses that seemed to complement the music.

As I fidgeted, still uncomfortable in the school knitwear, trying to accustom myself to his smell of cigarettes, clean shirt and something else I couldn't define, the boy pulled me closer.

"What's your name?" he asked.

Close up, I saw the shadow of long eyelashes — eyes that were hazel or green, I couldn't tell. I'd never been this close to a boy before. "Er, it's Carol," I gulped. "Carol Sheldon. What's yours?"

His smile deepened. "Michael," he said. "Michael Evans. Will you be 'ere next Friday night, Carol?"

Before I could answer, Janice, having left her partner, was at my side. Her face full of anxiety again, she nodded frantically towards the door. "That clock says it's quarter to ten, Carol!" she pointed out. "We'll 'ave to run if we'm to catch that bus!"

Next day, Saturday, I went with Mom and Dad to Great Bridge as usual to get the weekend shopping. After parking the car in Slater Street, Dad disappeared into the "Stork" for a couple of pints while Mom and I made our way to the butchers, cake shop and Adams, the big fruit and vegetable shop in the centre of the town.

"Wake up, our Carol — yo'm like a mawkin today!" Mom finally snapped, exasperated by my dreamy expression. "Now pick them taerters up, or we wo' 'ave time to go to the market!"

On the open air market outside the old Limerick pub, she chatted to the man who sold ladies' jumpers and cardigans. The prosperity of her evening job meant she had money to spend on such luxuries, and her green eyes shone as she began to sort through pastel coloured garments, all made of the latest man-made fibres.

"Ere — this is nice!" She pounced on a smart blue jumper with a peter pan collar. "I'll 'ave this!" Next to the black top was a white one, short sleeved and just right for bopping and I tore myself away from my secret dreams about Michael Evans long enough to pull a wistful face at it.

"Put this in an' all, please, Barney." Mom raised her eyebrows at my squeal of joy and passed the white top across the stall. "I'll never 'ave any money while I've got yo!" she grumbled good naturedly, fastening down the flap of her purse and handing the paper bag, with both garments in, for me to carry. "Now let's get back. Our Dave'll be in for 'is dinner before we know it!"

On the short drive home, I rested my head against the leather smelling upholstery and closed my eyes, the murmur of my parents' conversation in the front seats seeming to be miles away.

Nobody at home had asked me for details of my first night out at the dance hall, content that Janice and I had caught the ten o' clock bus back to Central Avenue, and not reported any trouble.

I was glad because it kept secret my dancing with a boy, and being asked, albeit casually, to see him again next week. As the disjointed words of the song we'd moved to swam in my dreamy head, I sighed, and began to sing,

230

"My only dream come true . . .

"My one and only you . . ."

"Stop that buzzin'!" Dad's swift command as he half turned his balding head took all the wind out of my sails and I tutted silently as I ruminated to myself that he had no Soul!

Soul was what Mr. Lynall had been telling us about last week, when he'd had us read yet again those strange poems of John Keats about the Eve of St. Agnes, and the Song of the Nightingale . . .

"Did yer 'ear what I said, Carol?" I started back to reality as the car drew to a halt outside our gate and Mom indicated that I should help her out with the bags.

"I'm sure that wench is goin' deaf!" she announced, as my brother and his new best mate, Sid, appeared with their fishing rods.

"Er's just saft!" Dave pronounced, and as we all trooped into the house. "Wot yer brought me from Great Bridge, Mom?"

"I aye brought yer nothin!" Mom replied, her eyebrows warning me to say nothing about my new white jumper. "But I got summat good to tell yer! Me an' yer dad've bin workin' things out, an' we reckon we can all go on 'oliday this year — to the seaside! — Ow about that, then?"

CHAPTER
FIVE

"MICHAEL EVANS'
    "CAROL SHELDON."

I wrote our two names on the inside cover of my exercise book. Then I carefully crossed out all the letters that were the same. "Love, like, hate, marry . . ." I scarcely saw Mr. Gilson, our history teacher sweep into the room until Sheila nudged me and scraped back her chair.

Standing with the rest of 5C, I felt my heart sink as I calculated that, according to the formula, Michael only "liked" me, while I was destined to "love" him. I sighed dramatically, and as Sheila stared at me, murmured, "Got somthin' to tell yer, at break!"

"When you've quite finished, Carol Sheldon!" At the front of the classroom, Mr. Gilson paused and glared at me, eyebrows raised in his sharp, intelligent face. "Heaven knows it's going to take a miracle, but I've vowed to get every one of you through your 'O' level history!" he reminded, yet again. "So pay attention, girl!"

"Yes, sir." Cheeks hot, I shut my exercise book just in case Mr. Gilson decided to dart up the aisle and look at it. As I shuffled in my seat, his voice began to boom enthusiastically about the impact of the Spinning Jenny on the Industrial Revolution. And it came to me very clearly, not for the first time, that I was living in two different worlds.

At break, the talk was all about where we'd been and what we'd done at the weekend. With Janice nodding verification at my side, I told Sheila all about our first visit to the "Con", culminating with my "creep" with Michael Evans.

"'E asked if I was goin' next week," I reported, as we all trooped, against the rules, into the girls' cloakroom and huddled for warmth behind the coats hanging above the painted bench. "So 'e'll probably be lookin' out for me!"

"I don't think 'e come in until after the interval, Carol, "Janice suddenly put in meaningfully. "An' that Tony 'e was with smelt of beer!"

"Well anyway," Sheila's interruption coincided with the ringing of the handbell outside the cloakroom door. "I was gonna ask you to come to my 'ouse next weekend, Carol. We can go to the dance "'all in Brownhills, an' the pictures, if yer like!"

As we trailed along to our next lesson on the other side of the big old house, she explained her suggestion that I go home with her by bus on the following Friday night and stay over until the Monday morning!

While Janice went to sit with her friend Mary, Sheila and I took up our usual places at the back of Mr. Lynall's English Literature class.

"I 'ope me mom says I can come, Sheila," I whispered, as the striking, moustachiod man entered the classroom carrying an armful of exercise book. "I think 'er will cos 'er's in a good mood. I day tell yer, did I? We'm goin' on we 'olidays in July. To a caravan in Rhyl . . ."

All sorts of thoughts jumbled together in my mind as the lesson began. Sheer excitement at the way my life and those of the people around me seemed to be opening up and changing. Dreams, never far below the surface, of becoming a writer one day, and seeing my name in print. And love, all bubbling up, just waiting to be given.

Mr. Lynall went around the class, handing back books and I felt my face go hot in remembered embarrassment as I thought back to a time, about twelve months before when, imagining myself madly in love with him, I'd deliberately written a poor essay!

In my mind's eye, as I scribbled unsatisfactorily in my cold bedroom, I'd seen him bending over Norma Dean's desk, giving her endless attention because, as she admitted herself, "English wasn't her best subject."

But to my horror, Mr. Lynall hadn't received my sub-standard work with anything like the tenderness I craved. Instead, he'd stood by the blackboard and hurled my book across the classroom in my general direction with the coolest, and to me most wounding of chastisements, "I expect better than this from you!"

"Well done, Carol!" Now, I received the compliment along with the book, and, opening the page to the end of my Mr. Polly essay, saw I had been awarded 65 per cent. "Some good writing here," Mr. Lynall had added. My spirits rose even higher.

When I got home that night, the talk was all about the prospective holiday.

"Our May's next door neighbour gid 'er the address for me," Mom explained, taking a piece of paper from behind the mantlepiece clock. "The camp's called ''Appy Lands' an' the confirmation come today. We'm all booked in fer the last wick in July!"

"I cor wait, Mom!" I explained, as I watched her gathering her things together for work. "An' talkin' of goin' away — my friend Sheila wants me to go an' stop at 'er 'ouse next weekend. Will it be all right?"

Mom frowned from me to the clock, which although still twenty minutes fast, meant she was cutting it fine if she wanted to catch her bus to the bakery. "We'll 'ave to ask yer dad, Carol," she said, distractedly. "Now dow forget the washin' up an' mek sure you both do yer 'omework!"

"'Ear that?" I told Dave bossily as soon as the door was closed. Though I might have known I wouldn't get my answer tonight, I'd been secretly hoping Mom would automatically support me in my request to go to Sheila's.

"Me an' Sid might be goin' on a trip!" My brother, infuriatingly, wasn't about to think about homework any more than I was! Sprawled on the sofa, he blinked at me in the eerie light of the television set he'd switched on the minute the back door closed. His lips smacked as he unwrapped a black jack chew and popped it in to join the mouthful he already had.

"We might be goin' all night fishin' — to Arley! Mom's gonna ask Dad about that, an' all!"

It would all work out fine, I told myself optimistically, as I later left him watching "Sea Hunt" and went upstairs to do my homework. Dad would agree to all our requests, and come the weekend, I'd be in Clayhanger with Sheila and her friends.

My only regret was that I wouldn't be at the "Con" and therefore Michael Evans would look for me in vain. But even that had its advantages, I worked out, blissfully writing my own story in my head.

By the time I went to the Wednesbury dance hall again, I'd be more used to the world of rock and roll. I'd appear as sophisticated and worldly wise as all the other impeccably turned out older girls Michael Evans had probably danced with there before!

"Car-ul!" Dave's voice bawled suddenly up the stairs. "It's Jo-un!" As I went, bleary eyed, across the half lit landing, he hissed: "Smelly Jo-un! Ere's 'ere again!"

"Shurrup!" I mouthed automatically down the stairs and pushed past him into the front room. There, Joan Hall was waiting, her grubby feet pushed into a pair of her mother's high heeled shoes, her school skirt embellished with a black waspie belt and her hair snatched back into a greasy pony tail that my nan would have said "showed where the tide had come in."

"Lo, Carol!" she beamed. "I've bin talkin' to Janice today, and' 'er says yo 'ad a great time at the dance! So I 'ope yer don't mind, but I've asked me Mom — an' 'er says I can come with yer — next time yer go to the 'Con'!"

236

CHAPTER
SIX

Sheila and I stood puffing cigarette smoke through her open bedroom window. And we just couldn't stop laughing!

"What a night!" Next door, we could hear Sheila's mom and dad talking as they got ready for bed. "Our Mom's face when that dopey Tony asked 'er if we'd gorra lavatory!"

"An' yo said — no, we dig an 'ole in the back garden!" We clung to each other, screeching in girlish glee as we recalled the moment we'd arrived home from the Brownhills dance hall with two soaking wet boys on rusty bicycles!

"Seriously, I've never known it rain so much," Sheila said, as she stubbed her cigarette on the window ledge and flicked it expertly out of the window. "Clayhanger's really flooded!"

"I know." Privately, I wondered why it had to rain quite so much the weekend I was away from home. Was it raining like this in Tipton, where my mom was dreaming about our planned summer holiday to Rhyl?

My friend closed the window on the squally scene and we silently got into our pyjamas. Only when we were sharing the three quarters size bed did the mirth begin again.

"Hey — that chap yo was with wore much brighter, was 'e?" I asked, leaning up on one elbow to look at Sheila's lively face. "'e dried 'is feet in front of yer mom's fire — then put 'em back in 'is wellies again — an' they was 'alf full o' water!"

"I know!" Sheila held her sides again as we both recalled the scene, "But the best bit of the whole night, I think was when you an' Tony fell over the chip shop wall!"

"I never expected that!" I agreed, rubbing my bottom where I had unceremoniously landed. "'e just come flyin' at me an' we seemed to tek off through the air!"

We rocked with laughter again, holding our sides while tears rolled down our cheeks. I'd never realised that boys could be so clumsy and clownish and supposed it was because Tony and his friend were the same age as ourselves.

Not like Michael from the dance hall, I thought dreamily, as I lay back down on Sheila's mother's spotless pillow case. He was mysterious and mature. I'd only met him once, but I already knew I'd never want to make fun of anything he said or did!

The rest of the weekend at Sheila's flew by, with her mom going to chapel and her dad busy in his shed before we all ate a huge Sunday dinner. In the evening, still drowsy from our lack of sleep, we sat around the fire and listened to "Sing Something Simple" on the radio.

"They don't like Elvis!" Sheila explained, embarrassed, as her mom got up to make a pot of tea and her dad adjusted the volume on the radio.

"It's all right," I whispered back, and as the melodious old songs filled the quiet room, found myself remembering the song my brother, mother and I used to dance to around the kitchen at 3 West Road. "Wilomenah is plump and round". The feeling of warmth and security would have been hard to put into words.

It was strange, next day, setting out for school from Sheila's, and I put my uniform on in her bedroom, relievedly buttoning my cardigan over my grubby white shirt. My rock 'n' roll skirt and petticoat I rolled up and pushed into my duffle bag.

Before we set out, Sheila took a blue chiffon headscarf out of her bag and tied it over her hair. "It's really windy today," she explained, "An' I'm going to youth club tonight, so I don't want me hair all ruined!"

There were three buses to catch and at each of the bus stops, a couple of teenagers on their way to the "Limes". None of them seemed to be having as much fun as Sheila and me, and we ignored them as we recalled our hilarious weekend, and commiserated with each other loudly about the school week ahead.

It was when we were in Walsall that Sheila suddenly went pale and grabbed my sleeve. "Oh no!" she gasped. "That car that just went past! I'm sure it was ol' Donithorne! And I 'aven't got me beret on!"

From beneath my own squashed beret, I stared at the pale blue headscarf which crowned so practically yet so incongruously her navy blue school uniform.

"E probably day see yer," I tried to encourage, as the bus came and we clattered onto the upper deck. "Dow worry about it!"

By the time we got to school, Sheila's scarf was tucked carefully away in her bag, and her beret perched temporarily on her head in the spot where it could do least damage to her hairstyle.

As we trooped into the prefabricated building that was the school hall for assembly, we were both trying to forget the trouble she might be in. If there was anything our rather eccentric head master was strict about, it was the wearing of school uniform, especially in sight of the general public.

The assembly was almost over, the customary rendition of the school hymn on the agenda that morning, when Mr. Donithorne suddenly rapped his fist on the lectern for attention.

"Now before we begin our day's work towards those all important GCEs of yours, I've got a treat for you all. Sheila Wilkinson — step to the front please!"

At my side, I heard Sheila gasp. I watched sympathetically as, head down, she moved reluctantly out of the back row of pupils and down the centre aisle to where the head and his staff were waiting.

You could've heard a pin drop as Mr. Donithorne instructed Sheila, "Now put on your head what you were wearing on your way to school this morning! Let's all take a good look at it!"

Horror stricken with embarrassment, Sheila just stared at him.

240

"Come on, girl — we haven't got all day!" he barked, his face flooding with dark, angry colour.

Sheila hung her head and mumbled that the scarf was in her bag, and I heaved a sigh of relief on her behalf.

But we might have known Mr. Donithorne wasn't going to be put off so easily.

"Then get it from your bag!" he roared, making everyone in the front row jump. "Then put it on, so that we can all see how the 'Limes' is being represented in the streets of Walsall!"

In abject misery, Sheila did as she was told, tying on the scarf with shaking fingers and biting her lip as she was forced to walk up and down through the rows of tittering, sympathetic, or just plain disinterested pupils.

"Perhaps, Miss Jones," the head master said in heavy sarcasm to Mfanwy, all fur coated ready for her first session of games. "We might think about incorporating blue head scarves into the school uniform — especially for those of our students who clearly have no brains!"

The games mistress raised her eyebrows and nodded politely, the assembly thankfully ended, and I followed Sheila into the nearby cloakroom.

"I hate him!" she stormed, wiping her hot face and damp eyes with the balled up scarf. "I really hate him!"

And in that moment, remembering the laughter and freedom of the weekend, I hated him too!

CHAPTER
SEVEN

It was February 3rd, 1959 — a school day like any other until the news filtered through.

"Buddy Holly's dead!" Sheila whispered to me, aghast, when we met in the cloakroom at break. "It was on the news this mornin'! There's been an aeroplane crash!"

"The Big Bopper an' Ritchie Valance was on it as well!" Barbara Phipps put in and as we looked at each other, I remembered our early rock and roll sessions in her dad's garden shed.

Barbara and I weren't close any more, and I'd heard a rumour she was thinking of leaving the "Limes" without taking any exams. But this bombshell about not one, but three of our heroes seemed to have brought us all together.

As the day went on, the feelings of disbelief and sadness persisted. The only person I had ever known who had died was Gilbert Miller, one of the 13 kids who had lived on the Lost City estate who had contacted diptheria at the age of ten.

I had obviously never met these three famous singers, but they were young too, and their music had changed the lives of countless kids all over the world! It all seemed so unfair and as usual when, feeling upset, I went to see my nan.

She was busy dressing small plastic dolls in crinoline dresses made of satin and lace, their legs first encased in a bag of old stockings and a cardboard base.

"Since yer grandad retired, e's bin goin' to the Sons of Rest," she told me the tale as usual, starting from the very beginning. "An' they 'ad a Christmas feet an' they was chargin' one an' eleven fer these dolls, so I 'ad a look at one an' figured out 'ow it was put together! Now, why're yer lookin' so down in the mouth, darlin'?"

I flushed and mumbled something as I reached for my tea, in its special china cup. Suddenly, it was really hard to put my feelings into words, and as if realising it, Nan put her work away and sat down beside me on the sofa.

Almost before I knew it, I was being transported by her stories to her own youth in Netherton at the time of the First World War.

"I was lucky — none of my brothers was called up. They was miners, see, an' in a reserved occupation, but we used to see the telegrams comin' — to say lads of 18 'ad been killed in France!"

"Did Grandad go to fight?" I knew the answer already, but I still liked to hear all about Grandad's adventures, which Nan could only repeat second hand. "'e tried to join up when 'e was sixteen, bless 'im!" she said fondly, shaking her head. "An' 'e got as far as Dover before 'e was told to go 'ome and join the boy scouts!"

"But 'e could've been killed?" As I made my thoughtful way home in the twilight, I tried to imagine a world where young men were expected to give their lives in the service of their country.

It put things into perspective, but it still didn't stop me feeling cheated because Buddy Holly was dead, and for the first time since it started, there was the slightest inkling. That rock and roll might not, after all, be around for ever more.

That Friday night, Janice, Joan and I set off to the dance hall together, our lips plastered with the white lipstick that had been free in "Valentine" that week, and our eyes widened by thick smears of black liner.

"Yo all look consumptive!" was my dad's verdict, as we passed him on the way to the bus stop. Then, he took another look at me, and his voice deepened into seriousness. "Be back on that ten o' clock bus, our Carol!" he ordered. "Or yer won't be goin' no more!"

Again, I had that sense of not knowing what to say — almost as if some awkward, sullen stranger had found her way into my body. So I mumbled a quick, unwilling assent, grabbed the arms of my friends and hurried off down the long road.

"My mom's said the same," Janice commiserated, when we got out of ear shot. "They don't want we to grow up — even though we'm 15 now, an' we could be at work!"

"Wish I was, sometimes!" I replied, while on the other side of me, Joan was proudly boasting that though she was only 14, her mom didn't mind what time she got home!

"I bet I could stop out all night if I liked," she said, as we reached the stop, where the bus was just about to pull out. "Our 'enry does it all the time! Er — c'n somebody lend me the penny fer me fare? I forgot me purse!"

As the bus travelled through the bleak, wintry streets, it picked up several people who were obviously headed for the same destination as us. Sitting on the back seat of the upper deck, with Janice beside me and a wide eyed Joan in front, I watched enviously as two girls in the latest fashions flounced up the metal stairs with two boys in Teddy Boy suits.

They all lit "Park Drive" cigarettes, and leant back, puffing out the smoke, laughing and joking as if they hadn't a care in the world.

They didn't have to bother with stupid rules about school berets, and as for G.C.E. "O" levels, they'd probably never even heard of them!

"What's up, Carol?" Janice looked across at me, her anxious face reflected through the dark window of the moving bus. "Yo'm very quiet tonight . . ."

"I bet 'er's dreamin' about that chap," Joan turned, grinning, as she pulled her pink bubble gum experimentally through her whitened lips. "The one 'oo catched 'er shoe over the school wall!"

"No, I ay!" I replied, truthfully. As the bus turned at last into the High Bullen, and drew to a halt at the place where we'd all get off, I pushed down my disgruntled, schoolgirl thoughts. And my spirits rose as I realised. Soon, if I was very lucky, I might be seeing Michael again!

CHAPTER
EIGHT

The dance was great, but Michael didn't come in until a quarter to ten!

"Dance?" he asked, appearing at my side and expertly breaking up the clumsy spinning threesome I shared with Janice and Joan.

"Missed yer last week," he went on, as I adapted my steps to his. Twisting under his arm, I smiled properly for what seemed the first time in ages.

"I went to my mate's for the weekend," I replied. My heart jolted as he raised his eyebrows, and I was momentarily glad I hadn't said "my mate from school."

As the strains of Elvis died away, to be replaced by Buddy Holly's "That'll Be the Day", I wondered if my curly haired partner would nod and move away to ask someone else to dance.

But Michael Evans obviously had no intention of doing that — a fact being noisily noticed by Janice and Joan from the edge of the dance floor! I turned, so that Michael shouldn't see Janice's grim finger pointing to the clock, reminding me mercilessly that it was less than 15 minutes till the ten o'clock bus!

"Shame about Buddy 'Olly," I said, as the now very poignant words filled the smoky air above my head.

"Yeah." Deftly, Michael twirled me round until our faces were only inches together in the spin. "My sister cried her eyes out! Still, 'er's only a kid — still at school!"

"Oh." I was glad that at that moment the record was changed even, even though out of the corner of my eye, I saw my two friends now jumping up and down with their coats over their arms. "I'll 'ave to go," I gabbled. "My mates want to get the next bus!"

"Let 'em go." Michael was holding on to my hand as the music changed to the now familiar "creep" songs. "I'll walk you 'ome," he offered, "You'll be all right. I promise."

I hesitated just for as long as it took to return the warmth and interest in his deep, hazelly green eyes. Then "O-Okay," I said, impulsively, "I'll just go an' tell 'em."

Janice's scandalised "tut-tutting," and Joan's embarrassingly loud squawk took them through the door of the dance hall and carried me back to where Michael was waiting, his arms out as if for a formal waltz as he drew me again into the strains of the Conway Twitty song I was already beginning to think of as 'ours".

One dreamy song followed another as we stumbled around the darkened hall, occasionally bumping into couples who were too engrossed in each other to notice.

"This is nice." Michael moved closer, his lips on my cheek, and I tried to relax and forget that the dimly lit clock above the door seemed to say ten past ten. By now, I realised, beginning to panic, the two J's would be

248

halfway home, and here I was, still in Wednesbury, with a lad I scarcely knew who had probably expected me to stay until the dance hall closed!

Luckily, though, after the next song, the lights came on again to reveal several couples, passionately kissing.

"They 'ave another interval now," Michael told me, as he adjusted his smart jacket. "We might as well go — if yer ready."

I tried not to show how relieved I was! If we walked fast, I calculated, as I darted towards the door, I could still be home before eleven, and maybe — just maybe — Dad would be in bed!

"I'll just get my coat!" I called over my shoulder. I was glad that on that particular night, Mom had persuaded me to borrow her old "swagger". It might not look right over the rock 'n' roll skirt, but it was warm and definitely more "grown up" than my gaberdine mack would've been!

On the long hike back to Tipton, Michael and I talked, or rather he talked, and I, for once, listened. By the time we reached Cox's Bridge, known locally as the "murder bridge," I had learnt that he was 18 years old and worked in a factory in Dudley.

"I live on the Priory estate," he said, walking with his arm around me as if he'd done it all his life. "There's Mom and Dad, me brother Terry an' me three sisters — but as I said before, they'm only kids . . ."

He shrugged as he said the words, and I again felt anxiety and guilt stir, deep inside me. He obviously thought I was the same age as himself, and I'd said nothing yet to disillusion him!

"Smoke?" He turned towards me, a packet of Senior Service in his hand.

I nodded. "Thanks." For a moment our hands were cupped together round the lighter flame. In the same light, I saw my wrist watch — a present on my tenth birthday.

"It's 'alf past ten!" I gasped.

Michael shrugged, waving an arm at the black, star studded sky. "Why, not got to go to work tomorrow, 'ave yer?"

"Er, no!" I quickened my steps, and heard myself go on: "But me dad as to be up early — an' — an' I've forgot me key!"

Nobody I knew had a key. That didn't happen until you were 21 — and sometimes not even then!

Reminded by a little voice inside me what a liar I had become, I began to run, and Michael, after a moment's puzzled frown, joined me! We ran all the way to Tibbington Terrace, and there I managed to persuade him to leave me.

"It's only round the corner — 'onest!" I gabbled, terrified that at any moment my irate dad would appear, and discover me with an unknown lad who now had both arms around me!

"I'll be okay now — you go an' get 'ome to Dudley!" Reluctantly, Michael let me go, but not before he had pulled me close and kissed me thoroughly on the lips!

My heart hammering, I heard him whisper: "See yer next wick, eh? Same time, same place!" Then I was flying round the corner, past the Unicorn pub with its

250

little groups of customers who had been saying goodnight since turning out time!

Pulling my mother's coat around me, feeling my thin bopping shoes splash through icy puddles which were part rain part factory oil, I ran even faster. By now, Janice and Joan were probably in bed. It was after eleven o' clock!

I stared at the little watch in the light of the nearest street lamp. If only it was ten past ten instead of ten past eleven, I thought. And it was then that I had my idea!

Feeling a bit like I'd been on a cross country run practice for real, I stood by our wall for a moment to get my breath. Then I carefully turned back the fingers of my watch an hour, tidied my ponytail, and made myself walk casually up the side of the house. Through my mind was going the memory of Mom once sending us out to school a whole hour early. And the clock on the mantlepiece that was always twenty minutes fast!

"Wheer the 'ell 'ave yer been?" Before I could get to the back door, it was wrenched open and Mom was standing there, the light spilling out over her slim figure, dressed in her nightie and coat.

Beyond her, perched wide eyed on the sofa, I saw my brother, feet bare, long legs dangling out of his worn blue pyjamas.

"What's 'e doin' up?" I asked, before I could stop myself. But I got no answer, because Mom was ordering me, with a silent finger, into the house.

Meanwhile, Dad, who had obviously been out looking for me, was hurrying along the side of the house. He glared at me as if he couldn't believe what I'd done.

"I told you — the ten o' clock bus!" he reminded me. "Otherwise, yer wouldn't go out again!"

"It — it's on'y just after ten!" Stupidly desparate, I held out my arm with the lying wristwatch strapped on it: "L-look!"

My parents looked instead at each other. While from the sofa, Dave groaned and buried his head in his hands.

"Ow saft d'yer think we am?" With a furious gesture, Mom pointed to the clock, which, unhelpfully, struck the single note of eleven thirty. In the firegrate beneath, the lump of coal left in for morning settled, but gave off no heat. I shivered.

"Nice try, Carol," Dad said, with a little shake of his balding head. "but it wo' wash! Yo've deliberately defied me — an' so yo' can stop at 'um Friday nights from now on! Yo can forget about the bloody dance 'all an' concentrate on yer school work instead!"

CHAPTER
NINE

"So yer won't be able to see Michael on Friday?" Sheila and I were sitting on the church wall and it didn't seem to matter if anybody went past and saw us with the cross country Woodbine.

I took a clumsy drag and coughed. At home it had been really miserable over the weekend, and I couldn't even run to my nan's because I knew she'd never approve of what I'd done.

The stroll back to school, followed by the high drama of panting and gasping back to where Mfanwy stood with her stopwatch had lost all appeal for me. And I barely nodded when the games mistress pulled her astrakan hat snugly round her ears and told us proudly we'd "done it" in eight minutes, this time!

"I'm really expecting great things of you girls!" she beamed. "I can't remember two such keen cross country runners in one class before!"

"What yer gonna do, Carol?" hissed Janice when she later joined Sheila and myself in the cloakroom. "Er's really expectin' yo'll win the race! An' ut's only a few wicks to Sports day!"

I looked at her anxious face and sighed. "That's the least o' me problems, Jan! Yer sin me dad's face when 'e come to your 'ouse on Friday night lookin' fer me! I cor see 'im ever lettin' me out again!"

By the next Friday night, I felt so desperate and wretched I resorted to writing poetry about Michael and myself being divided by a chasm. Pouring out the words on a piece of scrap paper, I shivered in my bedroom, hearing the buzz of the television below, and knowing the whole family was gathered round it.

It didn't help knowing that Janice and Joan would already be on the bus to Wednesbury, and their evening of freedom and fun. By the time Mom came up the stairs with a mug of tea, I was standing glaring out of the dark landing window. Wishing with all my heart that I could just fly through it!

"Yer might as well come down," Mom began as I automatically took the drink from her. "Yer dad'll come round quicker if yer don't seem to be sulkin'. An' we've just bin talkin' about the 'oliday!"

Reluctantly, I followed her down to the living room, where Dad and Dave sat on the sofa with a brochure between them.

"'Appy Lands Caravan Park!" My brother announced. "There's an amusement arcade — a fair — an' a fish' 'n' chop shop!"

"Yo 'ave to look a bit happy to get in there though, our Carol!" Dad put in as I squeezed in between them. Then he looked straight at me. "Think yer can manage it?"

I paused, biting my lip as I thought of all the things that seemed to be conspiring to make me less than happy lately. The two different worlds of school and home — the great divide between independent workers and immature school kids. And most of all, the imposition of being here, with my boring family, when I should be out, rock and rolling with a boy who had kissed me on the lips! Then, I looked at Dad again, and saw that he was smiling!

"I should be able to manage it," I said, taking a long drink of sweet tea and pulling the holiday brochure almost casually towards me. "We ay goin' till the last week in July, am we?"

The next day, I longed to seek out Janice and Joan to find out what had happened at the "Con" the night before. But Mom had other plans.

"I want to go up Dudley," she said, as she unhooked the shopping bags off the back of the verandah door. "Our May says it's a good market on a Saturday! An' yo' can come with me, our Carol, to 'elp carry the bags!"

I opened my mouth to protest, as usual, that it was always me who had to carry shopping bags, and never my brother. But as Mom raised her eyebrows, I realised that, in my present circumstances, it wouldn't be a good thing.

"Yer dad's already said 'e'll drop we off," Mom went on encouragingly, pulling on her coat and handing me my hated school mack. "So we'll only 'ave to get the bus one way!"

In spite of myself, I brightened up as we drove down Central Avenue and onto the main road. The last time we went to Dudley, a year or so now, Mom had taken me into a wonderful café place called Flemings, where we sat on a bench and ate some faggots and peas that were nearly as good as my Nan's homemade ones. Maybe if I was lucky and we got the shopping over and done with . . .

The market stretched along the high street, with the ornate fountain at one end and the public toilets at the other. We bought potatoes and cabbage, then apples and the bananas which, with bread and butter, would make up our Saturday tea.

"Ere y' are, Carol!" Mom handed me the heavy vinyl bag before she opened her purse. "Wear the young 'uns out fust, eh?" she grinned at the weatherbeaten man behind the stall. Then, as if relenting, she nudged me and pointed ahead.

"Look — there's a book stall! Want to 'ave a look?"

I blinked in surprise. Mom had told me more than once that old books, like old clothes "carried germs" and that was the reason we didn't have them in the house. But now, here I was, with my shilling pocket money in my purse, a whole row of books, and permission to look at them!

I had just paid for an edition of the complete works of William Shakespeare, a bargain at elevenpence, when a familiar female voice shrilled:

"Ello, Liza! I thought it was yo!"

Mom and I both turned to see Mrs. Phipps and Barbara — resplendent in a matching dress and jacket, her auburn haired piled on her head, and her feet warmly and fashionably clad in suede boots edged with fur!

"Ello, Gladys," Mom replied pleasantly. Oblivious to my swift mortification, she hoisted the potato bag back into my arms and placed the Shakespeare on top, right under my chin. "Goin' somewhere nice?"

"Already bin — ay we, cock?" The little woman beamed at her glossy daughter who in turned, smirked at me. "Our Bar's got a job — apprentice at Cynthia's hair modes — just off the arcade!" she said, proudly. "'er can start on Monday, now 'er's turned 15! Two guineas a wick, an' a day in 'airdresser's school!"

"College, mom! It's college!" Barbara corrected, while I tried to take in the amazing fact that the rumours I'd heard about her leaving school were true. "But I'll be learnin' summut useful — fer a change!"

Her condescending look took in my school mack, the lumpy vegetable bag and the incongruous book of Shakespeare's plays, jammed under my chin.

Yo should gerra job as well, Carol!" she said. "Earn yerself a bit o' money!"

"Money ay everythin!" It was exactly the sort of thing my Nan would've said, and I turned in surprise to see Mom pursing her lips as she began to lead the way along the cobblestones of the market. "Come on, cock. Let's go an' ave a bit o' dinner!"

As we later pushed our way into the warm, aroma filled back room of the faggots and peas shop and found a seat on the worn bench that we could both squeeze into, she smiled at me thoughtfully:

"Fancy that Barbara leavin' school!" she said. "Showin' off about 'er posh job!"

I nodded, concentrating on the busy waitress who was coming to take our order. Mr. Donithorne wouldn't be pleased to learn Barbara had left school so abruptly, I thought. Seeing our mercurial headmaster in my mind's eye, I felt again the mixed emotions that had come when he shamed my best friend Sheila over the silly blue headscarf.

It was a relief when, bellies full, Mom and I got on the bus to go home. Now I could find my friends and catch up with all I'd missed the night before at the dance hall!

I needn't think about school until Monday morning, I told myself gleefully — though I might spend Sunday afternoon reading a bit of The Merchant of Venice in my huge, unopened book.

It was noisy outside Joan's house, even with the door closed. As I knocked I could hear the sound of raised voices, and a blaring radio, interspersed with the wild yapping of the mongrel dog they kept on the back yard.

"Shurrup!" yelled Joan, as she opened the door. She peered out suspiciously, then her face cleared with recognition, and barely concealed excitement:

"Hey, Carol!" she said, closing the door on the commotion. "I talked to yer chap last night — yer know, Michael! 'E day know 'oo I was at fust, but then I tode 'im. Me brother's 'Enry 'All — an' me an "you go to the same school!"

CHAPTER
TEN

"Get that down yer!" My Nan said staunchly, as she placed the piled-up plate of shin beef, onions and potatoes in front of me. "Before yer faerther comes!"

It was a joke, I knew, one of her old Netherton sayings like the one about eating while there was a good light! But I felt a flush come to my face as I sat at her red formica table. As I realised that for the first time ever, I wouldn't feel comfortable if my dad walked in Nan's house right then.

As it was, I couldn't be absolutely sure that he hadn't already told her about my staying out late and telling lies about my watch.

Nan sat down opposite and we spent the next few minutes in a busy companionable silence that culminated as usual in her passing me a rather battered tin dessert spoon from the cutlery drawer. 'Ere — drink yer gravy! That's the best bit!"

I grinned, relaxing, able to forget about both my bad day at school, and my thwarted social life. "Hey, Nan!" I said, brightening even more as I pulled a slip of paper out of my tunic pocket. "We'm all goin to the pictures — to see *Hamlet*!" I pored over the details, all written in Mr. Lynall's dashing hand. "English Literature film trip. Tuesday 8th March. Odeon theatre, Wednesbury!"

"Oh?" Nan frowned as she gathered up our plates and went to put the kettle on. Then, her imagination seemed to seize on the most interesting of my words, and she said, "I went to the theatre once — well, it was the Op'ra 'ouse, really. In Dudley!"

I frowned, watching her take a homemade cake from the bright red tin. "Where's that, then?" I asked, puzzled. "Mom an' me went to Dudley on Saturday, but I day see any Opera 'ouse!"

"That's cos it ay theer anymore — I think it burnt down!" Nan told me, looking up from cutting the cake. "There's a picture 'ouse therabouts now — the Plaza, I think it's called!"

"Did you see an Opera then, Nan?" I was truly amazed she'd never mentioned this phenomena before.

"Oh, I never went in!" Nan looked positively scandalised as she rattled the china cups into their saucers. "It was all a trick, see, of yer grandad's sister, Martha — a real bad 'un 'er was, if ever there was one."

With silent, mutual accord, we left the washing up and went to sit in front of the fire with our tea and cake.

"It was durin' the first war," Nan told me, wriggling about until she got comfortable. "Yer grandad was away fightin' fer king an' country, but 'is sister day like me, an' 'er decided to tell 'im I was no better than I should be!"

260

I wasn't sure what that meant, but now wasn't the time to ask. "Go on!" I urged.

"Well," Nan slurped her tea and narrowed her eyes. "'Er wrote to me to ask me to meet 'er outside the Op'ra 'ouse this one night. Well, my mother day 'old with them plerces, so I 'ad to tell lies — sayin' I was goin' to my pal's down the road, an' then catch the tram into Dudley!"

I picked up my cake, aware of an uncomfortable feeling of familiarity the story was causing me to have. "So — was Martha waiting for yer?" I asked.

"Huh! Was 'er 'ell!" Nan replied. "No, 'er let me walk up an' down outside that Op'ra 'ouse, then 'er wrote an' tode yer grandad I was a street walker — tryin' to get off with men!"

I stared at her open mouthed, and she shook her head as if she still couldn't believe it herself. "But there was wuss to come," she went on, unbelievably. "I got on the next tram back to Netherton — an' me mother knew wheer I'd bin. 'Yo've bin to the Op'ra 'ouse, our Madam!' her said an' though I tried to deny it, 'Yo ave-, 'cos Mrs. Marsh next door but one sez 'er 'usband's sin yer on 'is way 'um from work'!"

You could never keep anything away from Nan's mother. I'd been told that before. But as I walked home that evening, the letter about *Hamlet* burning a hole in my pocket, I realised, not for the first time, there wasn't much you could keep away from my nan, either!

At school, all the talk was about leaving — who was and who wasn't staying on until they were 16. In assembly, Mr. Donithorne paced the floor, and finally, in exasperation, hit his forehead with the flat of his hand, and declared, "You know, my parents came up from Cornwall last weekend. I went to the railway station to see them off and you'll never guess what — the train came in!"

"What's he on about?" At my side, Sheila muttered her dislike and distrust and I didn't blame her. But as I stared at the almost manic figure in front of us, I realised suddenly what he meant.

It was all about being reliable. In coming to the "Limes" and beginning the intensive G.C.E. course, we had all made an unspoken promise to try that bit harder to prove we weren't absolute failures. Just because we hadn't passed our eleven plus.

"Twelve months!" Mr. Donithorne was repeating now. "It'll be over before any of you know it! And all you have to do during that time is what's expected of you!"

"That dow sound like much fun!" I said behind my hand to Sheila. I sighed as we all stood up to sing the school hymn "These things shall be! A loftier race than all the earth has known, shall rise!"

The trouble was, I thought, fidgeting and sighing, I wasn't sure I wanted to be part of a "loftier race" any more! I just wanted to be allowed to go out to the dance hall again. And find out if Michael Evans was still speaking to me!

CHAPTER
ELEVEN

"All right, yer can go!" Dad conceded that Friday night I had both dreaded and longed for, "But I want you on that ten o' clock bus without fail — an' no more lies or playin' silly buggers with watches!"

"I promise!" Jumping up, I hugged him before dashing towards the stairs. "Thanks, Dad!"

Within seconds, I was changed into my rock 'n' roll outfit and flying through the house towards the back door. Calculating the time by our inaccurate clock, I realised my two dancing friends would be on their way to the bus stop by now.

Thinking again of what Joan had told me about her conversation with Michael, I felt my face go hot. I hated the thought of his knowing I was like his kid sisters and "just a school girl", and yet, if he really liked me, it surely shouldn't make that much difference! And at least I'd have an excuse to go home with my friends, the way I should have done the last time we met!

By the time the bus got to Wednesbury, I was a bundle of nerves and both Joan and Janice commented on my uncharacteristic quietness.

"I reckon 'er's thinkin' about 'er chap again, ay yer, Carol?" Joan's bony elbow dug into my side as we all linked arms and turned the corner of High Bullen. "An' theer 'e is — look! Michael! Michael — over 'ere!"

While Janice tried unsuccessfully to "shush" Joan, I turned away in mortification, staring unseeingly down Union Street. Meanwhile, across the road, walking into the nearest pub with two other young men was the object of all my secret dreams, and the inspiration for all my tortuous poetry!

"Michael — Carol's 'ere!" Just as I thought Joan couldn't get any more embarrassing, she proved me wrong. Seizing me by the arm with her pincer like fingers, she almost dragged me under the lamp light. "Ay yer gonna speak to 'er?"

As his companions stood back watching him, Michael Evans just turned in our direction and frowned. In the lights of the pub doorway, I saw his curly hair, the lips that had, only two weeks ago, met mine in the promise I had dreamt about ever since.

Then he drew himself up, adjusted his flecked jacket on his broad shoulders, and followed his friends. Totally and crushingly ignoring my very existence.

"Dow worry, Carol — e'll probably ask yer to dance, later on!" Janice tried to say encouragingly as the three of us fell into step again, Joan's face full of puzzlement.

"Huh — 'e needn't bloody bother!" I replied. "I wouldn't dance with 'im again — not now!"

And I really tried not to care when, at nine thirty that night, Michael and his friends came into the dance hall, and he made a beeline for a tall blonde who was obviously in his own age group.

Back at home that night via the ten o' clock bus, and basking momentarily in Mom and Dad's approval, I told myself I'd finished with men forever. Or at least until Joan Hall had stopped coming out dancing with me!

The prospect of going to the cinema during school hours still excited me, and as Mr. Lynall waxed lyrical about the Laurence Olivier's *Hamlet* we were all about to see, I felt my heartbeat quicken.

"Wish it was Elvis!" murmued Janice at my side. "'e was in that film at the Rialto last wick an' everybody cried! E dies in the end!"

"So does Hamlet!" I wanted to say, but didn't quite have the nerve. Since my cruel rejection by Michael Evans, I'd been secretly reading Shakespeare's play in my icy bedroom while my parents were at work.

"To be or not to be . . ." Ignoring my brother's disbelieving snorts from the landing, I'd spoken the words aloud. They went straight to the heart of so many dilemnas in life, I ruminated, sagely. "Whether one should leave school at 15 and get a job — or stay on — and face the slings and arrows of the dreaded GCCs . . .!"

"Hey, Carol — did yer know Margaret Turner's leavin' school — today?" Janice whispered, as the bell rang and we collected our books to go to the next class. "'er was cryin' er eyes out in the cloakroom this mornin!"

I stopped dead, remembering the happy day I'd spent with Margaret and her many brothers and eccentric Gran. At break, I went to look for her, and found her in the garden, huddled miserably on a bench behind the most secluded beech tree.

"What's up, Margaret?" I asked, as she bunched her hankie in her hand and raised her tear stained face. "Janice Smith says yo'm leavin'!"

"That's right, Carol," she nodded. I sat beside her. The noise of the other pupils seemed to be part of another world — one she was no longer part of. She sighed. "Me mom's avin' another bab, an' they need me to go to work! I c'n get three quid a wick in Osbourn's offices. I start on Monday!"

"But what about your history?" I asked, shocked and appalled as I contemplated all she would be giving up. "Yer wanted to do an "A" level in that — an' there's them lovely poems in the school magazine. I know you write them!"

Margaret smiled as our eyes met. "They'm nothin' much," she said, "That's why I just use me initials. As for the history — well, me dad says I can still study that when I've left. There's a big library in Wolverhampton!"

The bell rang again and we looked resignedly at each other. "It's been nice knowin' yer, anyway, Carol," Margaret said, "An' the best o' luck with yer exams — an' yer stories! Yo'm good at them!"

"Thanks, Margaret." I squeezed her arm and we went our separate ways, her to her last school history lesson, me to Commerce which I was still certain would last into eternity.

By the time I came out of the Odeon cinema next afternoon, I had definitely made up my mind. I was staying on at school, if only to have continuing access to great works of literature like the one I had just enjoyed. — Though "enjoyed" was hardly the word!

"You all right, Carol?" Janice peered at me as we made our way to the bus stop. "You seem miles away!"

"S'pose I am!" I mumbled, embarrassed yet still not wanting to talk. How could I tell her I was still with the tragic prince Hamlet in his haunted castle in Elsinor?

Recalling the fine language and gestures of the play, I quivered, not for the first time, with the knowledge of an author's power. If only I could write something one day that would make people laugh and cry — make them hold their breath, turn pages and forget about what was happening in real life!

The only way, I could see it now, was to work hard at school, especially with the English literature and language in which I knew I excelled.

"Come on, Jan!" We jumped on the waiting bus and clattered up the stairs to our usual place on the front seat.

But though I tried hard to listen, and even exchanged school news and pleasantries with my friend, I was still secretly "miles away" in my own secret dreams.

The euphoria lasted right until the moment I walked into our house, and Mom, on her way out to the bakery, announced "Oh, Carol, I'm glad I've sid yer before I go! I've bin out an' got yer a job, cock! At Woolworths, down Great Bridge!"

CHAPTER
TWELVE

"It's on'y a Saturday job!" My brother filled me in with the details Mom had obviously been discussing before I came home. "Yo'll get 12 bob a wick!" He pulled an envious face. "Wish I was old enough to go!"

"Yo'm welcome to it!" I muttered through my teeth, as Mom waved and disappeared out of the verandah door. While I was relieved the unexpected work wasn't full time, I certainly didn't relish the thought of spending every Saturday from now on behind a counter in Great Bridge Woolworths!

Mom had arranged for me to go and see Miss Williams, the manageress, prior to starting work on the Saturday. A thin, efficient looking woman, Miss Williams wore her blue overall with pride and peered suspiciously at my duffle bag full of books.

"You'll be on electrics," she told me with some satisfaction. "Nine to six, ten minute break mid morning and afternoon. One hour precisely for lunch."

Maybe it wouldn't be so bad after all, I began to tell myself optimistically as the week went by. Mom was only going to take six shillings of my twelve, which would leave me more pocket money than I'd ever owned.

"You can save up for yer 'olidays now," she suggested on the Thursday night as we sat by the fire with our suppertime cake and cocoa. "An buy some of the new clothes yo'm always moanin' about! Yer might 'ave to stop goin' to this Friday night dance, though — if yo'm to get up on Saturday mornings!"

"I'll be all right!" I assured her. She shook her head and said she'd "see". And momentary panic shot through me at just the thought of missing my now regular outings to the "Con".

Not only had I learnt to bop really well, able to twirl both Joan and Janice under my arms at the same time. There were loads of other boys who now asked me to dance, so that I scarcely noticed whether the superciliously older Michael Evans was on the premises or not!

Saturday morning, Mom dragged me out of bed at a quarter to eight. "Yo'd best 'ave a good wash down, an' put some talcum powder under yer arms," she advised. Taking a kettle of hot water into our frozen bathroom, she emptied it into the washbasin, then hurried downstairs to refill and boil it.

"Huh!" Already it felt like an "examination by the nurse" kind of day! I shivered in my thin pyjamas longing for a mug of hot tea, wondering why, if we had to go to all this fuss for Woolworths, Mom hadn't banked the fire up so that I could have a proper bath!

By the time I was on the half past eight bus to Great Bridge, I was feeling thoroughly disgruntled! Following the instructions I'd been given by the manageress, I went to the side entrance of the familiar brick building, and up the flight of stairs to where I'd had my interview.

There I stood and watched, feeling like a duck out of water, while women of all ages and sizes took blue overalls out of a huge metal wardrobe and carefully put them on.

"You the new Saturday girl then?" The young woman looked across as if only just noticing me. She was tall and slim, with very high heels and a chic blonde hairstyle and make up that made her look like a model in a magazine.

I nodded. "Yes, I'm Carol," I gulped. "Er — I'm on electrics, I think."

"Oh." My companion looked at me with a slightly worried frown. Meanwhile, everyone else was hurrying down another set of stairs which led, I knew, to the shop floor. "Best find you an overall. I'm Joyce, by the way." There was a little, meaningful pause. "Cosmetics."

A few moment's later, I found myself standing by the electrics counter. A huge display of items which were all totally mysterious to me, it ran the whole length of one wall. At one end were lampshades, and the other, rolls of lino.

"You're responsible for selling the lampshades and for measuring and cutting the lino," the waiting manageress told me with the air of one conferring a great honour. "Plugs, wire, adaptors, everything is priced and labelled. Now, I'll show you how to use the till!"

"Er — where's the lady — you know — who works 'ere all the time?" I asked nervously. Miss Williams's deft, manicured fingers paused as she demonstrated via "No Sale" how the huge black till worked.

She put one finger up to her neatly pencilled eyebrow and smoothed it absently as she lied, "She'll be in later today. Now, we're getting a little queue — so I'll just stay here while you serve your first few customers!"

"I couldn't believe it!" I told Sheila the following Monday lunchtime, as we queued for dinner outside the prefab that was the "Limes" school dining room. "I waited all day, gerrin' more and more in a muddle, an' the woman 'oo works on electrics never come in at all!"

"But everybody else did?" Sheila had already heard a few of my woes, mumbled in a break in history. We shuffled forward a few more feet in the queue. "Yer mom and dad?"

"An' me nan!" I groaned aloud as I recalled Nan's beaming smile, as I tried unsuccessfully to ring up two and elevenpence for an adaptor.

"My grand-daughter!" she'd told the customer, who, infuriated beyond words, had asked me for what he wanted three times and then finally snatched it, muttering, off the wall display. "It's only a Saturday job, to 'earn 'er a bit of pocket money! Er's clever — at the County Commercial School, y'know!"

"Nan wanted to know why they 'adn't put me on a nice counter, like cosmetics!" I told Sheila with a sigh. "'er day know that's where everybody thinks they should be! But the very wust thing, Sheila, was when me bloody brother come in — just as I was tryin' to measure out the lino!"

Again my mind went back to Saturday, when, in the middle of the frantic, confusion-filled afternoon, the thing I'd dreaded happened. A well-dressed man and woman, who had stood comparing colours and patterns for a while, came up to me.

"We'd like three yards of the blue and white check linoleum, if you please, miss," the man said.

"Er, right," I swallowed, and picking up the wooden yard rule and huge scissors, led the couple back to the lino display. The roll was heavy, but somehow, I wrestled it off the stand and onto the floor. I got on my knees and took hold of the stuff, bulky end of the roll, then, moving along with the wooden rule, I tried to place it on top of the moving bulk.

"It just kept rollin' back up!" I told Sheila, as our eyes met in a moment of complete understanding. "I day like to ask the man an' woman to stand on it cos they was so posh, an' I thought any minute Miss Williams'd come along an' see me. Then I looked up from among the feet — some more people 'ad stopped to see what was goin' on — an' there was our Dave an' 'is mate Sid from the grammar school — doubled up, killin' themselves laughin' at me! I'll tell yer summat Sheila, I cor imagine anythin' worse!"

CHAPTER
THIRTEEN

The ice lollies were the best I'd ever tasted. And I'd promised to buy Joan Hall one too if she walked up the road with me.

"We make 'em ourselves see," the man in the little shop at the top of Wood Green Road turned from the fridge and neatly decanted a second orange lolly from the little wine glass. "Pure orange pop, that is!"

I dug deep into my mack pocket and handed over four pennies. Soon, Joan and I were walking again, sucking as we went, past Wednesbury library, then the Odeon.

"Me brother was on the wireless again last night," Joan lied opportunely. 'Enry 'All's Guest Night. Did yer 'ear it?"

"No." I shook my head, and hastily changing the subject, sighed. "It's the Sports day next Wednesday! That's why I'm tryin' to walk a bit. I dunno what me and Sheila's gonna do!"

My heart sank at the thought of setting out, in full view of everyone, across the muddy playing fields where the annual sports event was held. As Mfanwy was forever proudly telling us, the course was over a mile, and visitors from other schools often came along to support and encourage. Sheila and I were really going to make fools of ourselves!

Joan looked at me almost shyly over the fast disappearing lolly. "Yo'll need to build up yer strength, Carol," she advised. "If I was you, I'd 'ave two dinners that day — like I do!"

"What d'yer mean?" I frowned. Joan sniffed and wiped her nose on the back of her hand before flicking the lolly stick expertly down the nearest drain.

"Well, I wouldn't tell yer if Janice was 'ere — but most days, I 'ave me dinner an' puddin — then I join the back of the queue an' go in the canteen again!"

I stopped dead in my tracks and stared down at her diminutive figure in the creased school uniform. She gazed back, undeterred.

"So today, you 'ad shepherd's pie, an' rhubarb crumble . . ."

"Then shepherd's pie an' roobub crumble . . ." Joan gave an impressive belch and hodged up her school skirt. "Come on, let's gerron the bus! I'm dyin' fer me tay!"

Over the next few days, I walked from the "Limes" into Wednesbury every afternoon, sometimes with my friends, but more often alone. It felt like it was doing me good, after being cooped up in stuffy classrooms all day, and I pulled off my restrictive beret and stuffed it into my pocket, glad to feel the fresh air on my head and face.

Spring was just beginning to put in an appearance on the buds of the trees I passed in Brunswick Park, and the adjoining cemetery, and as I walked, I mentally wrote a poem, taking a leaf out of Margaret's book:

"Spring is here, Spring at last!
Saying goodbye to a winter that's past!"

It wasn't good enough, I knew to go in the school magazine with just my initials. But it was the best I could do for now.

I looked across the road at the Edwardian houses on Wood Green Road. Some of them had three storeys, and seemed like great mansions to me. I wondered what it must be like to live in a house like that, with high ceilings and plenty of space.

I'd have my own library, I dreamt, with all the books I'd ever want to read, and more. And a proper study, with a desk, and a typewriter like we used in our classes at school, except that it wouldn't have all the letters blacked out ... I'd read enough books to know now that most writers couldn't touch type anyway — in fact, the most famous ones seemed to do it with just two fingers!

Sports day dawned, another bright, springlike day that made me think of open spaces and the seaside, which I'd be seeing for real when the family went to Rhyl at the end of July.

Clad in our navy shorts and aertex shirts, Sheila and I shivered and muttered. And tried without success to avoid the games mistress's beckoning blue eyes.

"I wish I 'adn't ad them two dinners!" I complained, only half acknowledging Joan Hall's encouraging wave from behind the starting line. "Liver an' onions it was — then rice puddin' . . ."

"Then liver and onions an' rice pudding. I know!" Sheila didn't look the least bit sympathetic. "Wish our mother'd believed I 'ad the flu — I wouldn't be 'ere at all, then!"

My own mother had refused to be taken in too, turfing me out of bed and out of the house with no sympathy at all.

"I'm writing no notes, Madam! Yo've bin pretendin' to practise all these months, so yo'll just 'ave to get among the others an' run!"

Her thin face had worn the same expression of grim resolution I had come to recognise every Saturday morning when she got me up unrelentingly to catch the early bus to Woolworth's electric counter!

"We cor always do what we want!" It was a philosophy she'd been faced with all her life, and now it was part of her. Fatalistic. Gritty. Real in a way I respected but instinctively shied away from.

"RUN!" From somewhere far away, Mr Donithorne himself blew the whistle. The whole school seemed to be there, and at least half of them were in the race.

My heart sank as I looked around the crowd, seeing keen faces and fit and sturdy limbs. After double liver and onions and rice pudding, my limbs seemed solid, and as Sheila and I tutted at each other, and began to

276

lumber along, I thought inconsequentially, about my new hero. *Hamlet*.

"O that this too, too solid flesh would melt . . ."

No-one had told us that the field would be this muddy, and as we moved fitfully forward, black mud splashed up the backs of our legs from beneath our squelching plimsolls.

"Yuk!" Sheila exclaimed, stopping to hold one sodden foot in the air. Then she looked around. "They'm all passin' us!" she said, unnecessarily.

Through the mist around me, I saw determined faces and flying feet as the crowd surged across the field. Turning, I saw Mfanwy Jones just staring at us, her eyes narrowed with disbelief or revenge. I couldn't tell which.

Left behind for ever now, we staggered forward, and Joan Hall, with a wide eyed Janice Smith at her side, darted up to us, faster than any of the contestants.

"Hey, Carol!" she beamed, pointing to a little group standing at the edge of the field. "That other chap's 'ere — y'know, the one from the 'igh school 'oo caught yer shoe that day over the wall! E's killin' imself loffin' at yer!"

"So day yer finish, then?" My brother helped himself to the last fig bar biscuit before darting through the verandah door to meet Sid.

"Course we did!" I pulled a righteously indignant face. "Mfanwy — Miss Jones — said we wouldn't get a point for the 'ouse, if we day!"

"Well, yer've come 'ome in a right state, I do know that!" Mom declared, picking up the basket she took to the bakery. "Just mek sure yo' get rid of all that mud 'fore I come 'ome!"

Left alone, I looked down at my muddy fingernails. Now the cross country run fiasco was over, I felt strangely flat, and the unspoken knowledge that Sheila and I wouldn't ever be allowed to skip games again was a sobering one . . .

Restless and lonely, I decided to walk to Nan's. People was coming home from work, and the streets were full of that eerie twilight glow that always made me think anything could happen.

"What brings you 'ere?" Nan asked the question that couldn't disguise her delight in finding me on the doorstep. "Come on in, darlin'. Yer grandad's just gone out bowlin'. They got a tournliment on!"

"Oh." I followed her into the living room with its familiar and welcoming clutter. "I've bin doin' sport meself today," I said, flopping down into the armchair in the corner. "That's why me legs am so muddy. Cross country run!"

"Well I never!" Nan sat at the table and automatically pulled the teapot towards her. The tin that held the homemade cake was, as always, at her side. "I knew yo' 'ad to do 'ockey 'cos I bought yer stick off Mrs. Arnold's girl," she said, "But runnin' across the country — that's summat else, ay it?"

"Oh ar." I sighed, and rubbed at another dirty fingernail. Nan edged the cup of tea and piece of cake across to me and soon, fortified, I was able to go into more detail.

"It was a mile, an' me an' me mate, Sheila got a 'ouse point each." I half closed my eyes as I remembered our two hot, uncomfortable bodies, and all those eyes. Particularly Mfanwy's eyes, while the fair haired boy from Wednesbury Boys High School held his sides and laughed until I thought he'd burst.

"Sheila come seventy second," I told Nan with a deep sigh, knowin she was the only person on earth I could confess all the details to at that moment: "And I — er — come seventy third!"

A slight, hesitant frown passed over my grandmother's love filled face. Then, she took a slurp of her tea and piped up, "Seventy third, eh? Well, that ay too bad, is it, darlin'? 'Ow many was in this race o' yourn then?"

For the first time that I could remember, I couldn't quite meet her eyes.

"Seventy three," I gulped. And in that deep flush of joy that came from knowing that the number didn't matter "Another cup o' tea, Nanna?"

Little Apples Will Grow Again

Fred Brown

Even in the snow and ice of winter, when snowballs flew, and cold and busy gloved and ungloved hands patted snowmen into shape, the parents and grandparents would gather, shiver and talk about the weather.

Fred Brown recounts his own boisterous childhood, and the earlier life of his parents, Syd and Mary. They met whilst both in service and, despite struggling with Syd's depression, raised a large family.

With five brothers and a younger sister, Fred's early years were full of noise and mischief. Whilst fraught with terror for the adults, the war provided numerous distractions for the boys, from air raids to collecting shrapnel. This, along with joining one of the gangs that roamed the surrounding streets, meant that the children were always occupied.

ISBN 978-0-7531-9462-1 (hb)
ISBN 978-0-7531-9463-8 (pb)

Southend Memories

Dee Gordon

The seafront in the 1950s was awash with day trippers, with trains into London running every ten minutes. There was hardly any traffic along the beachside roads apart from coaches and buses.

Southend Memories is the unique and fascinating result of many conversations with the residents of the town, recalling life in there during the 1950s and '60s. Vivid memories are recounted — focusing particularly on social change. As well as schooldays, work and play, transport and entertainment, there are also memories of the late '60s clashes between Mods and Rockers, of the infamous Wall of Death at the Kursaal, and of excursions to the longest pier in the world.

ISBN 978-0-7531-9458-4 (hb)
ISBN 978-0-7531-9459-1 (pb)

Aintree Days

Alexander Tulloch

If the sound of Sunday was church bells, the smell of Sunday was cabbage.

Alexander Tulloch effortlessly evokes life in Liverpool from 1945 to 1962, when he was growing up with his parents, sister and grandparents in a small terraced house in Aintree. He conjures up a world, to today's children as alien as Victorian England, in which all adults seemed to smoke for England, a pint of beer cost a few pence, where frost painted patterns on the inside of windows every winter, where the "lav" was a trek across the yard and where you always went on holiday to Landudno — an exciting 60 miles away.

ISBN 978-0-7531-9430-0 (hb)
ISBN 978-0-7531-9431-7 (pb)

For What It's Worth

Bryan Kelly

I was a fledgling Liver-Bird fluttering its unaccustomed wings, ready to soar blindly into the beckoning future, unaware of its apparent pitfalls and dangers.

Bryan Kelly was born in 1931. His father was a docker, and he and his seven brothers and sisters grew up in a tiny terraced house in Anfield. Although life for Bryan and his family was hard, he recalls his time growing up with great fondness. With recollections of schooldays, local characters, wartime (and particularly the Blitz), church activities and recreation, as well as anecdotes from day-to-day family life, this book is sure to conjure up many nostalgic memories for all those who know and love the city of Liverpool.

ISBN 978-0-7531-9412-6 (hb)
ISBN 978-0-7531-9413-3 (pb)